Northampton in the Late Middle Ages

The Archaeology and History of a Midland Town

E. T. Jones, J. Laughton and P. Clark

Centre for Urban History
University of Leicester

Working Paper No. 10

First Published in 2000 by the Centre for Urban History, University of Leicester.

Typeset in Times New Roman using Microsoft Word 97; printed and bound in England.

British Library Cataloguing-in-Publication Data.
A catalogue record for this book is available from the British Library.

ISBN 1-870664-20-5

MAP OF LATE MEDIEVAL NORTHAMPTON

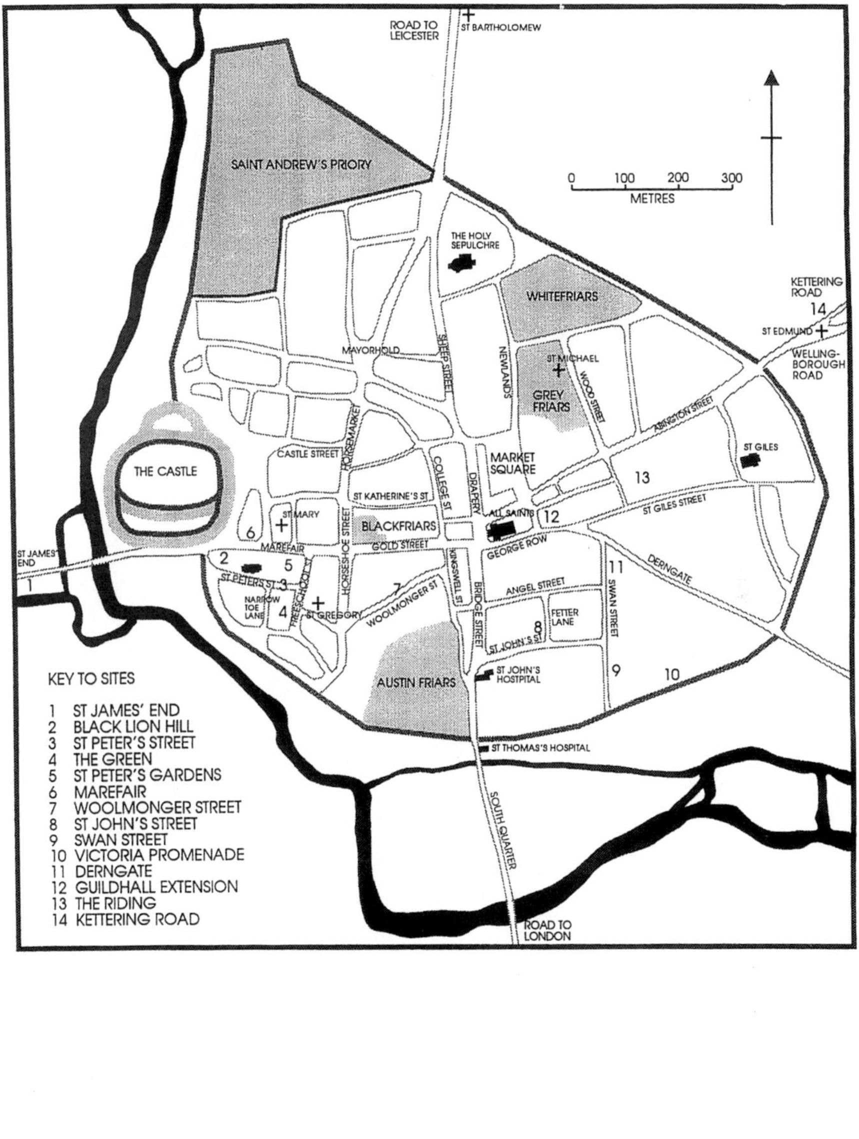

Acknowledgements

The research for this paper was conducted as part of the ESRC funded project 'Urban Hierarchy and Functions in the East Midlands in the Late Middle Ages' (R0002359022), 1995-97. The project was co-directed by Prof. Peter Clark (Centre for Urban History, University of Leicester), Dr Annie Grant (School of Archaeology, University of Leicester) and Prof. Chris Dyer (School of History, University of Birmingham). The principal authors of this working-paper, Dr Jane Laughton and Dr Evan Jones, were research officers on the project. Dr Neil Christie and Dr Deirdre O'Sullivan (School of Archaeology, University of Leicester) provided additional support and advice to the research team.

This working-paper could not have been completed without the active support, advice and assistance of various institutions and individuals in Northampton and elsewhere. Particular thanks are due to Mike Shaw (formerly Northamptonshire Archaeology, currently English Heritage Small Towns Project, Cheshire), Glenn Foard (regional archaeologist, Northamptonshire), Dr Jim Galloway (Centre for Metropolitan History, London), Dr Trevor Foulds (Nottingham Museum Service), Lord Ralph Kerr, and Northamptonshire Record Office.

Abbreviations

Early Will Register	Northamptonshire Record Office, 'Northampton Early Wills, 1467-1510'
LRO	Leicestershire Record Office
NBR	C.A. Markham and J.C. Cox (eds.), *The Records of the Borough of Northampton* (Northampton, 1898)
NRO	Northamptonshire Record Office
PRO	Public Record Office
RCHM, *Northampton*	Royal Commission on Historical Monuments, *An Inventory of the Archaeological Sites and Churches in Northampton* (HMSO 1985).
VCH	*Victoria County History*

INTRODUCTION
Peter Clark

According to John Leland's brief description in the 1530s, Northampton stood on the north bank of the Nene, 'Al the old building of the toune was of stone, the new is of tymbre...there is a faire suburbe withoute the South gate: and another, but lesse, withoute the Weste gate'.[1] Although the town suffered in the late sixteenth and early seventeenth centuries from a string of social problems (rising poverty, recurrent outbreaks of plague, an inrush of poor rural migrants, and a proliferation of petty alehouses), from the later Stuart period it enjoyed considerable affluence as part of the general urban renaissance of the 'long' eighteenth century. In the 1690s Celia Fiennes praised Northampton as 'a large town well built, the streets as large as most in London except Holborn and the Strand, the houses well built of brick and stone, some all stone, very regular buildings'.[2] Of particular note were the new town hall and other civic and domestic structures constructed after a major fire in the 1670s. Thirty years after Fiennes visited the town, Daniel Defoe commended it as 'the handsomest and best built town in all this part of England' with a famous horse trade and splendid great inns. Presiding over a local hierarchy of small market towns, with a clear role as an administrative, social and service centre for the shire, and with its economy consolidated by a strong boot and shoe industry, Georgian Northampton became, as Alan Everitt suggests, an affluent county town. This role as a middle-rank county town has in large measure determined its urban trajectory into the late twentieth century.[3]

---

[1] L.T. Smith (ed.), *The Itinerary of John Leland* (London, 1907), vol. I, 7.

[2] *NBR*, vol. II, 177-80, 233-9, 301-5 ; C. Morris (ed.), *The Journeys of Celia Fiennes* (London, 1947), 118.

[3] D. Defoe, *A Tour Through the Whole Island of Great Britain* (London, 1962), vol. II, 86; A. Everitt (ed.), *Perspectives in English Urban History* (London, 1973), 10-13, 92-137 *passim*; *idem*, 'Country, county and town: patterns of regional evolution in England' in P. Borsay (ed.), *The Eighteenth Century Town* (London, 1990), 97 *et seq*.; for a less rosy view of Northampton see A. Dyer, 'The Midlands' in P. Clark (ed.), *The Cambridge Urban*

Northampton's medieval development was more complicated and problematic, however. Re-established by the Danes about the end of the ninth century, it was already a major town by the time of the Domesday Book, exploiting its pivotal position in the kingdom half way between Winchester and York and between the East Coast and the Welsh Marches. After the Conquest, the Norman Senlis family built a large castle and town wall, and two important religious houses were established. It became a national political centre. In 1131 Henry I held a council there at which the barons swore fealty to Maud, a succession of great councils met at the town, and there were numerous royal visits. The town also benefited from the growth of a specialist high-quality cloth industry.[4] In 1184 Northampton bought the fee farm from the Crown and five years later obtained its first charter from Richard I. Under Henry III it acquired a further raft of privileges. Oxford students came after 1238 and a university was briefly established there in the 1260s.[5] In 1268 Edward I and his nobles assumed the cross at Northampton before going on crusade. In 1283-84 Parliament assembled in the town and in the early fourteenth century several more parliamentary sessions took place there. By this time Northampton was a leading provincial centre with considerable borough privileges and a prominent ecclesiastical position.[6]

By the 1320s, however, the town's political significance was in decline, the castle was in decay, and the cloth trade seems to have fallen away. Northampton's medieval heyday was clearly over, but the scale of its declension and the nature of the urban response is less certain. A number of other major urban centres in the

---

History of Britain, vol. II (Cambridge, 2000); C. Brown, *Northampton 1835-1985* (Chichester, 1990).

[4] *VCH, Northamptonshire,* vol. III, 1-2; C.A. Markham (ed.), *The Records of the Borough of Northampton,* (Northampton, 1898), vol. I, xvi-xviii; J. Bolton, *The Medieval English Economy 1150-1500* (London, 1980), 153.

[5] A.P. White, *The Story of Northampton* (Northampton, 1914).

[6] *VCH, Northamptonshire,* vol. III, 2 *et seq.*; *NBR*, vol. I, xviii *et seq.*; H.G. Richardson, 'The Schools of Northampton in the 12th century', *English Historical Review,* 56 (1941), 595-605.

Midlands experienced something of an economic free-fall in the later middle ages. Lincoln, a large city famous for wool and cloth trades lost a third of its population between 1377 and 1524/5, a decline which continued into the Elizabethan era when Lambarde spoke of it as 'little better than...a common market town'.[7] Another prominent Lincolnshire town, Stamford, saw its population slide from about 5,000 before the Black Death to perhaps 2,000 in the Tudor era, as its commercial position dwindled.[8] At the close of the medieval period Coventry suffered a catastrophic collapse of population, in part at least due to the problems of its broadcloth industry; here, as at Lincoln and Stamford, decline only seems to have been reversed during the late seventeenth and eighteenth centuries. Did Northampton follow a similar pattern of major crisis and only belated revival? Or was there a more limited down-turn and early recovery as the population figures – about 2,800 inhabitants in 1377 and 3,100 in 1524/5 – might suggest?[9]

Up to now Northampton has attracted relatively little attention from the new generation of urban historians working on the medieval and early modern town. Apart from the contributions by Alan Everitt on the Georgian period, other work has been limited. This is particularly so for medieval Northampton. On medieval Northampton the principal survey remains that by Helen Cam in the *Victoria County History*, published in 1930, which is principally concerned with the topography of the town.[10] J. H. Williams' *Saxon and Medieval Northampton* (Northampton, 1982) is short and focuses on the early medieval period. The rest of

---

[7] *NBR*, vol. I, xxvi *et seq.*; A. Dyer, *Decline and Growth in English Towns 1400-1640* (London, 1991), 74; P. Clark and P. Slack, *English Towns in Transition 1500-1700* (London, 1976), 25.

[8] A. Rogers (ed.), *The Making of Stamford* (Leicester, 1965), 49 *et seq.*; Dyer, *Growth and Decline*, 73.

[9] C. Phythian-Adams, *Desolation of a City: Coventry and the Urban Crisis of the late Middle Ages* (Cambridge 1979), chs. 1-3; for the decline of Lincoln, Stamford and Coventry see also C. Dyer and T.R. Slater, 'The Midlands' in D. Palliser (ed.), *The Cambridge Urban History*, vol. I (Cambridge, 2000).

[10] For the Everitt articles see note 3. *VCH, Northamptonshire*, vol. III , 1-67.

the specialist literature is largely confined to a few articles.[11] Again the town appears only intermittently in general studies, though, in the debate about urban economic decline in the late middle ages, Northampton is usually cited in the roll-call of declining places, albeit without much clarification or explanation.[12]

Northampton's slender historical press is due, in part at least, to the loss of civic records through major fires in 1516 and 1675. The latter, in the centre, also destroyed many of the town's vernacular buildings and thus seriously damaged the town's standing building evidence for its medieval development. At the same time, there remain important sources for the town, as is evident from *The Records of the Borough of Northampton* edited by C. A Markham and J. C. Cox, published over a century ago.[13]

The present double study by Evan Jones and Jane Laughton presents the authors' research findings and conclusions on the development of late medieval Northampton. Although this working-paper does not pretend to be an exhaustive study of the town, it offers a new more detailed perspective on it through the combination of a wide range of historical evidence (civic, probate, and London sources) with archaeological data, including hitherto unpublished findings from excavations in the town over the last twenty years. The work on Northampton was carried out as part of a wide-ranging examination of the urban hierarchy of the East Midlands in the late middle ages, funded by the Economic and Social Research Council and directed by Christopher Dyer (University of Birmingham) and Annie

---

[11] See Richardson, 'Schools'; M. Jolles, *A Short History of the Jews of Northampton* (Northampton, 1996).

[12] E.g., C. Phythian-Adams, 'Urban Decay in Late Medieval England' in P. Abrams and E.A. Wrigley (eds.), *Towns in Societies* (Cambridge, 1978), 166; also S. Reynolds, *An Introduction to the History of English Medieval Towns* (Oxford, 1977), 156. For the debate see: Dyer, *Decline and Growth*. For a more up to date account, drawing on this project's findings, see: Dyer and Slater, 'The Midlands'.

[13] *NBR*, vol. II, 3-4.

Grant and Peter Clark (University of Leicester).[14] The project's aims were to chart the broad pattern of the urban hierarchy in the East Midlands during the late middle ages; to identify, using a sample of communities, the principal economic, social and environmental markers for different levels of towns; to identify linkages between town and countryside; and to try to establish a new methodological framework exploiting both archaeological and documentary sources.

The project developed out of a strong feeling among the team leaders, reflecting a wider view among historians and archaeologists, that a more integrated approach of the two disciplines might not only help to overcome evidential lacunae but also could generate new ideas and interpretations concerning the late medieval town. The methodological significance of the project is discussed elsewhere, but in the detailed research on individual centres it became clear that an integrated approach generally worked best for the larger urban communities, such as Northampton and Leicester.

The analysis of Northampton that follows sheds valuable light on many detailed aspects of the late medieval town. But five points seem to be of especial general importance:

1. Urban population decline in late medieval Northampton did not occur uniformly. In much of the central area dense occupation continued through the period, while, as at Leicester, there may have been a realignment of the residential zone away from the western area which became more industrial.
2. Despite its decline in national significance, the town remained fairly prosperous, as indicated by the refurbishment of religious houses and parish churches (though some like All Saints and St Giles may have done better than others), by the extensive number of fraternities, and by road improvement.

---

[14] ESRC project 'Urban Hierarchy and Functions in the East Midlands in the Late Middle Ages' (R0002359022).

3. In the late fifteenth century the urban economy managed to replace its old staple industry, textiles (albeit dyeing remained important) with the growth of the tanning industry.

4. There was an important development of the service industry, as indicated by the increase of inns and consolidation of retailing with a profusion of permanent shops by about 1500. Here custom from landowners was significant with a number holding property in the eastern part of the town. Northampton's commercial links with an ascendant London were also influential.

5. Civic identity was maintained and reinforced in the period through civic buildings; some improvement to urban amenities such as waste disposal and water supply; and through the acquisition of new borough privileges (The 1489 Act reorganizing town government at Northampton and Leicester was vital for both towns).

Overall one's impression is that before the Reformation Northampton had already managed to redefine its role in the urban hierarchy, away from its earlier rather exceptional political prominence, towards a more stable and secure position as a middle-rank county town, serving an increasingly expansive agrarian region by the Tudor period. In this sense the town's later Georgian affluence had at least some of its foundations at the close of the middle ages.

THE ARCHAEOLOGICAL EVIDENCE

Evan Jones

The archaeological study of the towns examined during the 'Urban Hierarchy and Functions' project employed a number of sources of evidence. These included modern excavation reports and standing building surveys, representations of towns in maps, photographs, prints or drawings and early descriptions of towns or buildings in them. All these records were used to build up a detailed picture of the material development of individual towns, in order to elucidate information about how the townscape and urban environment changed in the late middle ages. To facilitate comparison between individual town studies, which was essential for what was primarily a regional study of urban development, a common approach and reporting style was adopted for all the towns examined. Since the nature and quality of the surviving evidence varied from place to place, some approaches were more useful than others in particular instances. Nevertheless, to illustrate the methodology employed in the project, and to reveal the strengths and weaknesses of the Northampton sources, all the approaches adopted in the project will be discussed in this paper.

From an archaeological perspective, Northampton's greatest weakness is its lack of standing building evidence. This is a result of two great fires, which devastated the town in 1516 and 1675. As a result, few medieval structures survive to the present day – or even survived long enough for early modern artists to depict them or commentators to describe them. It is thus impossible to carry out a detailed study of existing medieval buildings, as is possible for Stamford, or to examine a significant corpus of pictures of former medieval houses, as is possible for Leicester. While the standing building evidence from Northampton is poor, the town is exceptional for the volume of data available from archaeological excavations. The quality of this data is a result of the long-standing interest that Northampton's archaeologists have had in investigating the history of the medieval town, the willingness of the municipality to support archaeological investigations, and last, but not least, the commitment of Northampton's archaeologists to analysing, publishing and otherwise making available the evidence they uncovered.

Following the same pattern as adopted in the other studies, the archaeological section of this paper will examine evidence of changes in the size and location of the town's population. It will then consider whether the inhabitants of the town were more or less wealthy during the late middle ages. The functions of the late medieval town will be considered and, lastly, the paper will examine what light archaeological evidence can throw on the extent of Northampton's marketing networks. To enable the town's late medieval urban development to be placed in some sort of context, the paper will begin by outlining how the town came to acquire the urban form it possessed at the start of the fourteenth century.

Medieval Topography

Northampton was established as a Saxon *burh*, or defended settlement and served as a royal centre from at least the eighth century.[15] By Domesday (1086) it possessed approximately 300 houses, suggesting a population of around 1,500 people. Although tiny by modern standards, its size and taxable wealth was sufficient to make it about the twentieth most important town in England. The defended portion of the late Saxon settlement was restricted to a sixty-acre circular enclosure bisected by Horseshoe Street. This was Northampton's main street, since the major north-south route through the town passed along it before crossing the River Nene at a point to the immediate south of the Saxon town. Although most of the populace would have lived within the defences, some suburban development beyond the north and east gates may already have begun by 1066.

---

[15] The evidence for Northampton's topographical development in the period to 1300 is summarised in: J.H. Williams, *Saxon and Medieval Northampton* (Northampton, 1982), 28-42.

After the Conquest the Norman Senlis family built a castle on the western edge of the town and by 1086 they had established a 'new borough', also known as the 'Newlands', to the east. By 1100 a much larger defensive circuit had been constructed around the expanded town, encompassing an area of 245 acres. This circuit corresponds to the position of the later walls and gave the town one of the largest defended areas in England – exceeded only by London and Norwich. Although the town certainly expanded rapidly in the late eleventh and early twelfth centuries (the tax it paid to the King tripled between 1086 and 1130), the new defensive programme appears to have involved a considerable speculative element, with much room being left for future growth.

The establishment of the new borough had a major impact on the topographical focus of the town. Following the town's eastward expansion, a new bridge was constructed over the Nene, so that the north-south road passing through the town now went by way of the Drapery and Bridge Street. Since this was the most important north-south road in England until the mid-fourteenth century, it is perhaps unsurprising that the Northampton section of it developed into the town's principal thoroughfare.[16] The commercial ascendancy of the new borough was further reinforced by the location of Northampton's main market in the grounds of All Saints Church. In 1235, a new open market place, which still operates today, was established slightly north of the church, consolidating the commercial pre-eminence of the new borough.

[16] It was only during the late middle ages that the southern section of the Great North Road (A1) became pre-eminent as the route north. Matthew Paris' mid-thirteenth century route map from London to Berwick indicates that the normal route north then went up the London-Carlisle road (A5) as far as Stony Stratford, before heading through Northampton and Leicester to join the 'A1' at Grantham. Until Edward II's reign (d.1327) royal parties also followed this route, or variants of it, when travelling north: J.F. Edwards, 'The transport system of medieval England and Wales – a geographical synthesis' (unpublished PhD, University of Salford, 1987), 37-45, 49; E.J. Parsons (ed.), *The Map of Great Britain circa AD 1360 known as The Gough Map* (Oxford, 1958).

The evidence to be discussed below will reveal that in the twelfth to thirteenth centuries the intra-mural space of the town gradually filled up with both domestic properties and those of religious orders. By the mid-thirteenth century, when the town was reaching the height of its medieval prosperity, minor suburbs were also developing outside the four main gates. Nevertheless, it is probable that some land in the back-streets of the walled town remained undeveloped at this time – for the demand for suburban land along main routes was generally greater than that for isolated intra-mural areas away from main roads and gates. As in other Midland towns, like Leicester and Nottingham, such back-street areas would have been occupied by stables, vegetable gardens and orchards.

By the start of the fourteenth century Northampton had acquired the basic street system that it would retain until its rapid growth in the modern era. The main reason for being interested in the town's fourteenth-fifteenth century development is that such a study has the potential to throw light on the nature and extent of 'urban decline' at this time. For some decades, urban historians have been concerned with the way that England's urban development was affected by the demographic crisis of the late middle ages, when first famine, and then plague, reduced the country's population by half. Whilst it is undoubtedly the case that most English towns experienced a population reduction during this time, the key issue for urban historians is whether this was a period of de-urbanisation – i.e. did a smaller *proportion* of England's population live in towns and did towns play a less important role in the nation's economy. Although a lack of quantifiable data means that it may never be possible to answer these questions directly, this paper will at least seek to establish whether Northampton stagnated as its population and political influence declined, or whether it remained a vital and evolving economic centre. To examine these issues, this paper will therefore look not only at how the town's topography was affected by population decline but how wealthy the town remained and how its economic functions / marketing networks changed during the period.

Population

There are three types of material evidence that throw light on the size and location of medieval urban populations. These are standing domestic buildings, parish churches and the excavated remains of medieval domestic properties. Of these, the greatest problems arise over the use of parish churches to study population change. This is because while the physical growth or decline of parish churches can often be linked to population change, other factors, such as external patronage, also affected their development. Nevertheless, when Leicester and Stamford were studied, it was noted that the physical development of urban parish churches correlated closely with other indicators of population change.[17] For instance, at Leicester it was apparent that the abandonment of domestic occupation in the northern part of the walled town, as indicated by excavations and domestic standing building evidence, was accompanied by the decline of the parish churches in that area. At both Leicester and Stamford it was also clear that while the churches in the centre of the towns continued to be developed during the late middle ages, there was a significant shift in the nature of this development. During the eleventh-thirteenth centuries the development of parish churches was characterised by successive phases of rebuilding and a great expansion of parochial space within them, as naves were enlarged and aisles added. Although many churches continued to be developed in the later middle ages, the expansion of parochial floor space ceased. Development instead concentrated on the beautification and adornment of the churches through the creation of new towers, spires, clerestories, porches, windows and chancels. The decay and disappearance of parish churches is thus taken as a sign of population decline within a parish, while the failure to expand parochial floor space of churches that continued to be

---

[17] E.T. Jones, 'Leicester's Development in the Late Middle Ages'; E.T. Jones, 'Stamford's Development in the Late Middle Ages' (unpublished working papers, CUH Leicester, 1997).

developed after 1350 is taken as evidence that, although the churches might have remained quite wealthy, the population of their parishes had ceased to grow.

Since the study of both parish churches and surviving domestic housing proved fruitful in the study of other towns in the East Midlands, a similar approach was adopted for Northampton. Given that fewer standing buildings survive in Northampton than at Leicester or Stamford, any conclusions will necessarily be more tentative, the intent merely being to see if the evidence from standing buildings fits with the more extensive excavated evidence from the town. Of the nine medieval parish churches of Northampton, only three survive. These are St Peter's, St Giles' and the Holy Sepulchre.

St Peter's Church – Located close to the castle in the heart of the Saxon *burh*, this is an almost entirely mid-twelfth-century structure with few later additions. By itself the lack of later growth might be taken as an indicator that the population of St Peter's parish ceased to grow in the twelfth century. St Peter's, however, appears to have been an unusual church during the middle ages. The RCHM study of the church notes that in the twelfth century it was arranged in three distinct parts. This form is quite unlike that of other parish churches of the period, but is similar to the arrangement of a conventual church. Since the church is also unusual for being exceptionally well built and richly decorated for a parish church of the period, it is probable that its primary purpose was not in fact parochial. Rather, it seems likely that it operated as a religious house attached to the nearby castle but with limited parochial functions. In this respect it would bear similarities to the church of St Mary de Castro in Leicester.[18] Such a parallel is interesting, but if this interpretation is correct it means that the development of the church cannot act as a reliable indicator of demographic changes in the town.

---

[18] RCHM, *Northampton*, 57-9.

St Giles Church – This was originally built in the twelfth century as an aisleless cruciform church with a central tower. Early in the thirteenth century the chancel was rebuilt, lengthened by 1.25 metres, and increased in width on the north side. At the end of the thirteenth century aisles began to be added to the nave. This work was initially halted after only one bay had been built on the south side of the church. It seems that this was a result of fears about the safety of the tower and chancel – for the tower was subsequently strengthened and some repair and rebuilding work was carried out on and around the chancel. Once this had been completed, and a chapel had been built on the north side of the chancel, work resumed on the aisles. Two bays were added to the south aisle and three corresponding bays were added to the north of the nave. After the aisles had been constructed, the transepts were rebuilt to form eastward extensions of the aisles. The work to expand the parochial space of the church was thus finally completed in the mid-fourteenth century.[19]

The Holy Sepulchre – This church was built in the early twelfth century in imitation of the Holy Sepulchre in Jerusalem. This involved the building of a circular nave with a small oblong chancel attached to it. In the thirteenth-fourteenth century the part of the church that was open to extension, i.e. the area around the chancel, was expanded through the construction of a much larger and longer 'chancel' and the creation of three arcaded areas adjacent to it. Two of these were built during the thirteenth century to the north and one was built in the early fourteenth century to the south.[20] Although these arcaded areas have been interpreted as chapels, they may actually have served to accommodate the growing parish population. This would have been possible if the circular nave was converted into a chancel, while the new additions became the nave to which aisles

---

[19] *VCH, Northamptonshire*, vol. III, 51-5; RCHM, *Northampton*, 61-4.

[20] *VCH, Northamptonshire*, vol. III, 45-8; J.C. Cox and R.M. Serjeantson, *History of the Church of the Holy Sepulchre, Northampton* (1897).

were later added to accommodate extra parishioners. Although this interpretation is not considered in twentieth-century discussion of the church's development, it appears to be consistent with Cox and Serjeantson's nineteenth-century study of the church, which the *VCH* account is based on. Their study describes the additions to the 'Norman chancel' as aisles and their suggestion that the church grew in size 'in accordance with the requirements of an increasing population' implies that they believed that the new aisles constituted parochial space off a former Norman chancel that had then become the nave. If this suggestion is correct, it may be that the nave only reverted to a chancel, with chapels off it, in the seventeenth century, at which time the northern arcade was demolished and the chancel itself was reduced in length. This interpretation would make the medieval development of the Holy Sepulchre more comprehensible in the context of developments in parish churches across the East Midlands at this time. The conversion of this area into parochial space is certainly not implausible, for when the Victorians were faced with the same problem of how to expand a round church, they adopted this solution – turning the chancel into the nave, rebuilding the northernmost aisle and building a new chancel to the east of the old one.

The evidence relating to the surviving parish churches of Northampton is more ambiguous than that for Leicester or Stamford. This is because only three of the eight medieval churches survive and considerable doubt exists about the functions of St. Peter's and the exact pattern of development of the Holy Sepulchre. Nevertheless, the evidence from the two surviving eastern churches, and the accounts of the size and splendour of the church of All Saints (which was destroyed in the fire of 1675), indicates that the population of parishes in the new borough grew substantially during the twelfth-thirteenth centuries. The lack of expansion in parochial space after the mid-fourteenth century suggests that the population of the whole town was at best stagnant from this time. Since the town lost five out of its original nine parish churches in the fifteenth-sixteenth century, a far smaller number of churches would have had to accommodate the town's population.[21] This suggests that the town must have undergone a substantial reduction in the size of its population during this period.

Turning to the evidence for domestic housing, it may be noted that while the study of Leicester was based primarily on evidence relating to standing buildings, or buildings that were standing until at least the eighteenth or nineteenth century, the evidence for Northampton comes almost entirely from excavation reports. This is because fires destroyed most of the medieval domestic buildings of Northampton during the early modern period. The worst of these was the great fire of 1675, but by this date it seems likely that the great majority of the domestic buildings would have been post medieval, for a major fire had previously devastated the town in 1516. As a result, the only domestic structures that have survived to the modern period are some medieval vaulted cellars, of which just one survives to this day.[22] This cellar is a fourteenth-century vaulted undercroft on George Row, immediately to the south of All Saints Church. Another cellar was located on the Drapery, until it was destroyed during development work in 1860. Before its destruction it was described as having 'groined arches of decorated architecture', which suggests that it was originally part of a fourteenth-century domestic cellar. This commentator further noted that 'At the south-west end of College-street, groined arches are still remaining in some cellars'.[23] The location of these cellars in the commercial heart

---

[21] St Michael's disappeared after the Reformation. St Bartholomew's appears to have lost its parochial status by the early fifteenth century and by the time of the Reformation it was a chapel, now re-dedicated as the chapel of St Lawrence, belonging to St James' Priory. St Gregory's was annexed to All Saints in 1556 and its church went into secular hands. St Edmund's had fallen out of use by the mid-sixteenth century, although it had separate incumbents as late as 1535. St Mary's parish was formally incorporated into that of the Holy Sepulchre in 1590: RCHM, *Northampton*, 378-80.

[22] RCHM, *Northampton*, 387-8.

[23] *Wetton's Guide Book to Northampton, and its Vicinity* (London, 1849). Republished by Victor Hatley (1969), 70-1. In his introduction to the *Wetton* volume, Hatley establishes that its author was Edward Pretty, a prominent local antiquarian with a particular interest in architectural form. His assessment of the arches can therefore be relied on.

of the town suggests that, as at Leicester, the high price of land at central sites had encouraged property owners to expand their properties vertically. Since these cellars all appear to have been fourteenth-century structures, it seems that there was still a high demand for land on the key commercial sites even after the population of the town had begun to decline.

The excavated remains that throw most light on population change in the town are those that relate to domestic occupation. Since there have been a large number of excavations at Northampton on street frontage sites, it is possible to get a fairly good impression of how the population of the town contracted during the later middle ages. The basic pattern of occupation is given below on a site by site basis. The location of these sites is indicated on the map at the front of this volume.

Black Lion Hill – This excavation consisted of a long, narrow trench that encompassed both the street fronts of Marefair and the west end of St Peter's Street. In the period 1200-1350 the plots were densely occupied with a stone house fronting on to St Peter's Street, another fronting on to Marefair and a slighter stone building partly filling in the space behind the Marefair house. Both the house on Marefair and the 'in-fill' building behind it were abandoned during the period 1350-1500. The house on St Peter's Street was certainly occupied until at least 1500 before being abandoned or destroyed in the sixteenth century.[24]

Derngate – Archaeological work in this area was limited to watching briefs and the excavation of a number of small trenches. Some of these were close to the main medieval street of Derngate and some close to the top of Swan Street (medieval Cow Lane). The trenches near Derngate uncovered two substantial medieval stone buildings. One of the buildings (Area E) went through at least two phases of

---

[24] M. Shaw, 'Excavations on a Saxon and Medieval Site at Black Lion Hill, Northampton', *Northamptonshire Archaeology*, 20 (1985), 113-138.

construction. Its deep stone foundations suggest that it had two or more floors. It had a tiled floor and a stone garderobe situated behind it.[25] Although this building could not be precisely dated, the presence of a stone garderobe makes it likely that it dates to the late middle ages, for before this date domestic rubbish was generally buried in backyard pits. The other building (Area Z) was built after 1350. It also had stone wall footings but, since these were less substantial, it seems likely that this was a half-timbered building over dwarf walls. In trench B, also located on Derngate, other buildings were identified that appear to have been occupied until at least 1500, for a stone-lined pit of sixteenth-century date was associated with one of them. The trenches dug close to the front of Swan Street uncovered less impressive remains. In trench 'A' an insubstantial wall associated with a series of clay floors was uncovered, which overlaid two ovens of thirteenth to fourteenth-century date.

Guildhall Extension – This site was located close to the commercial core of the late medieval town. Since nineteenth-century cellars had destroyed all archaeological deposits in the vicinity of the medieval street front, excavations concentrated on a block of land between eight and twenty metres back from the road. The excavation revealed that the area was occupied from the twelfth century. By the early thirteenth century the site had undergone two phases of building work with the construction of at least two post-holed timber buildings and a possible boundary ditch running at right angles to St Giles Street. Sometime after the mid-thirteenth century the ditch was replaced by a stone wall, located three metres further east. This may have been a boundary wall but, since the wall had gaps in it, it is equally possible that the whole site was part of a single property with the wall merely serving to divide the domestic buildings to the west from an 'industrial' yard to the east. On the western side of the property a stone-founded building was constructed

[25] M. Shaw, 'Excavations on a Medieval site at Derngate, Northampton', *Northamptonshire Archaeology*, 19 (1984), 63-82.

in the late thirteenth century. This was clearly part of a substantial structure, since at least three rooms were identified and what appeared to be a two metre wide stone-floored passage ran along the east side of the building. As the building's walls were one metre thick, it is likely to have been of at least two storeys, of which at least the ground floor would have been of stone. To the east of the 'boundary' wall was an open yard in which a number of ovens were located. One of these appears to have been a drying-oven, which suggests that this was part of a bakehouse or brewhouse at this time. The western building and its associated features underwent various modifications before being abandoned in the second quarter of the sixteenth century. It is possible that this was connected with the great fire of 1516, which destroyed a large part of the town. Nevertheless, after a brief hiatus, the site was once more developed and was then intensively occupied until modern times.[26]

Kettering Road – This excavation consisted of two small trenches in the eastern suburb of St Edmund's End. One trench (A/B) examined a strip of land close to the street-front of the modern Kettering Road. The other trench (C) was located further back and ran at right angles to the first trench. The site was first developed in the twelfth-early thirteenth centuries when timber structures were erected in A/B and two small semi-cellared structures were constructed in trench C. The timber buildings in trench A/B were replaced in the mid-thirteenth century by a stone-founded building aligned along Kettering Road. The narrowness of the building's walls (c.0.75 metres) suggests that it had a dwarf stone wall supporting a timber superstructure. This building underwent a number modifications before being

---

[26] M. Shaw, 'Recent work in medieval Northampton: Archaeological excavations on St Giles' Street, 1990, and at St Edmund's End, 1988', *Northamptonshire Archaeology*, 27 (1996-7), 104-11, 139-40.

abandoned around the end of the fourteenth century. After this 'garden-soils' built up over the site and it remained unoccupied until the nineteenth century.[27]

Marefair – This site was located on the north side of the street opposite St Peter's Church. In the twelfth-thirteenth century the front of the site was occupied by a large stone building that could have been part of a terrace. Deposits within the house demonstrate continued occupation of the building until at least the later thirteenth to fourteenth century but it is uncertain whether it continued to be occupied after this. There was, however, continued development in the backyard area until the site was abandoned in the fifteenth-sixteenth century.[28]

Mayorhold – Fragmentary remains of a fifteenth-sixteenth century stone-founded building were found that post-dated an earlier structure.[29]

The Riding – This site lay in the curtilage of Gobion Manor. The medieval features were fragmentary but included two wall foundations and a number of pits. The large quantity of tile, which included Dutch imports of the late fifteenth century, and two pieces of architectural moulding suggest that a building of some pretensions was located here during the middle ages. Sometime between 1470 and c.1550 a small stone-founded structure was built on the site. This had heavy foundations and a floor of pitched stones set into hard mortar. To the south of this structure was a stone-lined well. These features appear to have remained in use until the early seventeenth century.[30]

---

[27] Shaw, 'Recent work in medieval Northampton: Archaeological excavations on St Giles' Street, 1990, and at St Edmund's End, 1988', 121-30.

[28] F. Williams, 'Excavations on Marefair, Northampton, 1977', *Northamptonshire Archaeology*, 14 (1979), 38-79.

[29] D.C. Maynard, 'Excavations on the Mayorhold, Northampton, 1971', *Northamptonshire Archaeology*, 11 (1976), 134-50.

[30] J.H Williams and C. Farwell, 'Excavations in The Riding, Northampton, in the Area of Gobion Manor, 1981-1982', *Northamptonshire Archaeology*, 19 (1984).

St James' End – Evaluations in this medieval suburb to the west of the town revealed two buildings fronting on to St James Street. One was a stone building with substantial foundations. It was built in the second half of the thirteenth century but appears to have been abandoned by 1300. Another building, built at about the same time, continued to be occupied and modified until the seventeenth century.[31]

St John's Street / Fetter Lane – This site consisted of a number of small trial trenches off streets lying behind the main medieval thoroughfare of Bridge Street. These trenches revealed the presence of timber buildings of twelfth-thirteenth century date followed by stone buildings of thirteenth to fourteenth-century date. There is no evidence of late medieval occupation in this area and since only 4 of the 1,325 medieval sherds found during excavations were dated to later than 1350, it seems fairly certain that these plots had been abandoned by the fifteenth century. As none of the thirteenth-fourteenth century tenement boundaries identified behind the street frontages correspond to post-medieval property boundaries, it is probable that the plots were amalgamated under one owner during the late medieval period.[32]

St Peter's Street / The Green – Excavations around St Peter's Street suggest that the road was first formally laid out and metalled between the late eleventh and thirteenth centuries. During this period both sides of the street were developed.[33] For the same period there is also evidence of occupation at 'The Green', immediately to the south. Most of the occupation evidence from this area consisted of pit digging, but a postholed timber building fronting on to Freeschool Street was

---

[31] M. Shaw and I. Soden, *Archaeological Evaluation of the former Travis Perkins site St James' End, Northampton, June-July 1996* (unpublished developer's report, Northamptonshire Archaeology, July 1996), 3-5.

[32] M. Shaw and S. Steadman, *An Archaeological Evaluation at St John's Street, Northampton, 1990* (unpublished developer's report, Northamptonshire Archaeology, October 1993).

[33] J.H. Williams, *St Peter's Street, Northampton. Excavations 1973-1976* (1979), 141-3.

identified from this phase and a similar building fronting on to Narrow Toe Lane was tentatively identified.[34] In the fourteenth century the whole of the north side of St Peter's Street was occupied by a number of stone-founded buildings but it appears that the south side was derelict at this time.[35] On 'The Green', the timber building fronting on to Freeschool Street was replaced by a stone one by the early fourteenth century and a stone-founded building was built on the site of the earlier timber house on Narrow Toe Lane.[36] Early in the fifteenth century there was a major redevelopment of both sides of St Peter's Street. The houses were of uniform construction and were all 8-12 metres long by 6 metres deep. Since this happened in one phase the excavator suggested that it constituted a single speculative development. A property was also built further up Freeschool Street in the late fifteenth century and a structure of uncertain date was tentatively identified behind this building during the excavation of St Peter's Gardens.[37] In the late fifteenth or early sixteenth century there appears to have been a major break in the pattern of settlement in the area. Evidence of burning in both St Peter's Street and The Green suggests that a major fire had destroyed many of the buildings in the area. The excavator associated this with the fire of 1516, which was said to have destroyed much of the town.[38] In a recent reinterpretation, however, it has been noted that if the fire came this late, it is difficult to explain the lack of Cistercian ware on the site.[39] One possible explanation for the lack of evidence of continued occupation after 1470 is that most of the houses may simply have been abandoned for domestic occupation in the later fifteenth century. This would fit with the

---

[34] M. Shaw, 'The excavation of a late fifteenth-seventeenth century tanning complex at The Green, Northampton', *Post-Medieval Archaeology*, 30 (1996), 72.

[35] Williams, *St Peter's Street,* 143-4.

[36] Shaw, 'The Green, Northampton'; Mike Shaw, pers. com.

[37] The medieval levels at St Peter's Gardens were only cursorily examined and broadly phased, since the excavators wished to concentrate their effort on the Saxon levels: J.H. Williams, M. Shaw and V. Denham, *Middle Saxon Palaces at Northampton* (Northampton, 1985), 27-8, 45.

[38] Williams, *St Peter's Street,* 145-7.

[39] Shaw, 'The Green, Northampton', 84-5.

evidence of House 4, which was one of the few houses on the street that had its backyard properly examined. This indicated that before the fire the northern end of the house had fallen into disrepair, a drain in the backyard had fallen out of use and a series of pits had been cut through the cobbled yard.[40] Some of these pits contained horn cores and cattle bones that suggest tanning and one contained iron tools that could have been used in leather working.[41] This house is one of the three houses on the street where the presence of significant amounts of Cistercian ware and other late medieval pottery types testifies to continued use post-1470.[42] The others are House 7 on Freeschool Street that must have been built post-1470 because the make-up of its walls contained Cistercian ware, and House 10 which appears to have changed function towards the end of the fifteenth century, for at this time its grain-drying oven was replaced by a tanning pit.[43] Very little pottery of post-1470 date was found at the other houses.[44] Since the entire area of St Peters Street / The Green was occupied by tanneries in the sixteenth century, and by this time there is no evidence of domestic occupation in the area, it is probable that the change in the area's usage from mixed domestic and industrial use to that dedicated

---

[40] Williams, *St Peter's Street,* 55.

[41] Shaw, 'The Green, Northampton', 100-1. Shaw apparently bases this on: Williams, *St Peter's Street,* 55-6, 189-90, 268, 271-3, 328-9.

[42] Nine sherds of Cistercian ware were found at House 4, indicating continued occupation post 1470: Williams, *St Peter's Street,* 190.

[43] House 7 contained 3 sherds of Cistercian in the lowest course of its wall and destruction debris contained a jetton of c.1520. At House 10, 69 sherds of Cistercian ware and 11 sherds of continental pottery dating to the late fifteenth century to early sixteenth century were found: Williams, *St Peter's Street,* 197-8, 215-16.

[44] Williams, *St Peter's Street.* Phase 6B at House 1 is said to be of late-fifteenth-century or early-sixteenth-century date. This is based on 1 sherd of Cistercian ware, out of a total of 40 sherds, relating to this phase: *ibid,* 137, 166-7. The continuation of occupation at House 2, post 1470 appears to be based on the presence of 2 sherds of Cistercian ware: *ibid,* 179. House 3 contains 1 sherd of Cistercian ware and 2 sherds of late fifteenth-early sixteenth century German stoneware: *ibid,* 185. Houses 5-6 contained too little pottery for it to be possible to phase the features but no Cistercian ware was found: *ibid,* 196. House 8 contained no late-medieval sherds: *ibid,* 205. House 9 was destroyed by fire. Destruction levels contain 2 sherds of Cistercian but also 1 delft - presumably intrusive from the seventeenth-eighteenth century occupation level above: *ibid,* 211.

to tanneries, predates the 1516 fire and possibly occurred as early as 1470. As tanning is a particularly noisome industry and many towns during the late medieval period legislated to move tanneries into non-residential areas, the main residential occupation of this part of the town may well have terminated in the latter part of the fifteenth century.

Swan Street (medieval Cow Lane) – During the middle ages this was a back street that led through the south-east corner of the town to river meadows lying beyond a minor town gate. The site lay close to the walls in an area well away from the main lines of commerce or commercial activity. The street itself seems to have been formally laid out in the thirteenth century and three insubstantial semi-cellared structures were built fronting on to it in the period c.1225-1300. These structures appear to have been similar to Saxon *grubenhäuser*. Settlement of the area was abandoned in the fourteenth century and cultivation deposits overlie the earlier levels. In the fifteenth century, structures of some type, possibly sheds or stables, were built on the site. Nevertheless, there is no evidence of domestic occupation at this time and by the sixteenth century even these ephemeral structures had disappeared, to be replaced by cultivation trenches associated with fragments of watering pots.[45]

Victoria Promenade – An evaluation on this site discovered evidence of a short-lived phase of occupation in the twelfth to thirteenth centuries in an area close to the town wall. After this the site was abandoned until the modern period.[46]

Woolmonger Street – Excavation trenches here were laid out to locate the front of houses situated on this medieval back-street. The excavations revealed that the

---

[45] M. Shaw and S. Steadman, 'Life on a Medieval back street: Archaeological excavations at Swan Street, Northampton, 1989', *Northamptonshire Archaeology*, 25 (1993-94), 127-58.
[46] M. Shaw, A. Chapman and I. Soden, 'Northampton', *Current Archaeology*, 155 (1997), 414.

street was formally laid out in the twelfth century and some timber buildings were constructed along it. These were replaced by stone structures in the thirteenth century and, during this period, new tenements were also laid out. The later development of the site is uncertain. At least one of the buildings had clearly been robbed of its foundation stones by the sixteenth-seventeenth century, indicating some decline in the intensity of occupation in the area. Nevertheless, the street was clearly not abandoned entirely, for a timber and stone building in trench 16 remained occupied until at least the seventeenth century.[47]

The evidence from the excavations conducted in the town suggests that Northampton was most densely occupied in the thirteenth century. By that time even the south-east quarter had been developed with evidence of domestic occupation on Swan Street, St John's Street, Fetter Lane and Victoria Promenade. In other parts of the town there also appears to have been a fairly intensive development with full occupation of the streets around St Peter's and evidence of in-filling behind the tenements at Black Lion Hill and along the length of Woolmonger Street. At the east suburb of St Edmund's End, there is evidence of occupation from the twelfth century. The west suburb of St James' End had also been colonised by the mid-thirteenth century.

In the late middle ages there was a contraction in the settled area of the town. During the fourteenth century, occupation ceased at St John's Street / Fetter Lane, the lower end of Swan Street, Victoria Promenade and Kettering Road. In other areas there is evidence of a decline in the intensity of occupation, even if settlement continued in some form. At Black Lion Hill, two out of the three buildings had disappeared by 1500, only one of the two houses identified at St James' End survived after 1300 and there appears to have been some decline in the intensity of occupation on Woolmonger Street. The most interesting aspect of the process of

---

[47] I. Soden, *Excavations at Woolmonger Street, Northampton*, (unpublished draft).

settlement retraction is that it did not occur in a uniform manner. The demand for land in the heart of the town seems to have remained high enough in the fourteenth century for property holders to build cellars along the main commercial streets. Occupation also continued at Derngate, the Mayorhold, The Riding, the Guildhall Extension and St James' End. The major excavations around St Peter's reveal continued dense occupation until the late fifteenth century.

During the late fifteenth or early sixteenth century, the domestic occupation of the three sites around St Peter's ceased, the last building at Black Lion Hill was abandoned and the occupation of the Marefair site came to an end. There is also a brief hiatus in the occupation of the Guildhall Extension, in the centre of the town, at this time. This decline may indicate a further phase of urban retraction during the early sixteenth century.[48] On the other hand, it should be noted that most of the sites discussed here lay in the western part of the town. Since tanneries increasingly dominated this area in this period, the apparent abandonment of domestic occupation in this part of the town may simply be due to relocation of the urban population away from what was becoming a particularly noisome industrial zone.

Wealth and Status

To examine the wealth of the late medieval town, the following section will examine parish churches, religious houses, municipal structures, domestic housing, service features and artefacts.

As was noted in the previous section, only three of Northampton's medieval churches have survived. Of these St Peter's shows the least sign of late medieval

---

[48] This has been suggested in a recent article by some of the town's archaeologists: Shaw, Chapman and Soden, 'Northampton', 415.

development, with only a couple of windows attesting to its fourteenth-fifteenth century maintenance.[49] Although this was not a typical parish church, the failure to improve and develop it can be contrasted with St Mary de Castro in Leicester, which had a clerestory and a new roof added to its great south aisle during the late middle ages. At the other Northampton churches, the most important late medieval developments were those at the Holy Sepulchre, where the round part of the church was raised and a west tower and spire were added in the late fourteenth century. About this time a tall gated niche was also inserted in the wall of the Round. This was probably intended for the keeping of processional crosses – reflecting the increasing importance of processional ceremony in the late medieval church.[50] At St Giles' the only improvement after the mid-fourteenth century was the addition of a fifteenth-century chapel.[51] Although the form of these late medieval improvements, i.e. additions of towers, spires, clerestories and chapels is typical of the period, the extent of the improvements, especially in the fifteenth century, is much more limited than at Leicester or Stamford. This may be because Northampton was particularly poor in the fifteenth century, but since only a few churches have survived it would be dangerous to base too much on the available evidence.

Of the religious houses of Northampton, only the hospital of St John's survives above ground. Although there is a great deal of modern work in the building, the original building was constructed in the fourteenth century before undergoing substantial alterations in the fifteenth century.[52] The spending of money on religious houses is also attested from the excavations at Greyfriars. The construction of the cloisters of this friary only began between the later thirteenth

---

[49] RCHM, *Northampton*, 57-9.

[50] Cox and Serjeantson, *Church of the Holy Sepulchre,* 45-50.

[51] RCHM, *Northampton*, 61-4.

[52] *VCH, Northamptonshire,* vol. III, 59-60. For Master's house, see *Associated Architectural Societies Reports and Papers,* 12 (1874), 225-30.

century and the later fourteenth century. The continued development of the site is testified by the re-tiling of the church floor in the fifteenth century and the rebuilding of the north-south cloister in the last quarter of the fifteenth century. During the fifteenth century the church floor at Greyfriars was also re-tiled.[53] Since depictions and descriptions of the now destroyed St Thomas' Hospital indicate it to have been a fifteenth-century stone building, it would appear that there was substantial expenditure on Northampton's religious houses until the very end of the middle ages.[54] This pattern of development is again closely paralleled to developments at Leicester and Stamford. Although the wealth of religious houses is not a very reliable indicator of the wealth of the general populace, since friaries and hospitals relied heavily on bequests from local townspeople, the development of the religious houses at Northampton does indicate that not everyone in the town was impoverished during this period.

Although none of Northampton's medieval municipal structures survive, there are early modern accounts and depictions of the fourteenth-century town hall (depicted on front cover). This was originally a two-storey ashlar-faced stone structure to which a third floor was added in the fifteenth century.[55] The building was finely built with a crenelated parapet. It was clearly built to be an impressive structure and one that was possibly harking back to a more glorious past when Northampton was a town of considerable political and military significance. Whether the reality of the late medieval town lived up to the town hall's front is debatable, but its fine features do indicate that there was enough money in the town for its burgesses to be able to make a fairly extravagant architectural statement.

---

[53] J.H. Williams, 'Excavations at Greyfriars, Northampton 1972', *Northamptonshire Archaeology*, 13 (1978), 96-160.

[54] *VCH, Northamptonshire,* vol. III, 60-1.

[55] *VCH, Northamptonshire,* vol. III, 36-7.

Studies of the town's domestic housing are limited by the lack of standing buildings. Nevertheless, excavations throw some light on changing building patterns, which give some indication of the changing pattern of wealth in the town. In general terms the thirteenth century was a period in which post-holed timber buildings were largely replaced by stone-founded buildings.[56] The early stone buildings frequently had heavily-built stone walls up to 1.2 metres thick. Since these walls were usually unmortared it seems unlikely that they could have been of two storeys, but it has been noted that they are massive enough to have been capable of supporting a wooden upper floor. The predominance of stone-founded buildings continued in the late medieval period, but fourteenth-fifteenth century walls were generally slighter – often only 0.8 metres thick. This change has been associated with the spread of timber-framed buildings resting on dwarf stone walls.[57] Whether such buildings mark an advance in architectural form or comfort over the thirteenth-century stone buildings is a moot point, but the timber-framed buildings certainly marked an improvement over post-fast structures that typified the housing of what is generally defined as the period of Northampton's greatest wealth. Beside these changes, it may be noted that the disappearance of the very poor quality semi-cellared structures on Swan Street after 1300 suggests a reduction in the size of the impoverished urban underclass that had been so prevalent in thirteenth century towns.

Apart from examining basic changes in house construction techniques, it may also be possible to infer something of the changing patterns of domestic wealth from

---

[56] Williams, *St Peter's Street*, 143; Shaw, 'The Green', 72; Soden, 'Woolmonger Street'.

[57] At Black Lion Hill and St James' End, buildings with massive stone foundations were directly superseded by buildings with the slighter walls probably built as a base for timber-framed superstructures: Shaw, 'Black Lion Hill', 121; Shaw and Soden, *Archaeological Evaluation of the former Travis Perkins site St James' End*, 6-11. At other sites it is simply apparent that late-fourteenth-fifteenth century walls were generally of slighter build, e.g. the Area Z building on Derngate and the foundation in Trench B: Shaw, 'Medieval site at Derngate', 75.

evidence of how houses were equipped. In terms of flooring it appears that even in the fifteenth century the houses of St Peter's Street still relied on basic floors of beaten earth or clay.[58] This is one reason for believing that the area was not a particularly wealthy one at that time. At other sites, however, there is evidence of more expensive floors being constructed. The best example of this is The Riding, where fragments of ceramic floor tile were identified as Dutch imports of thirteenth-fifteenth century date.[59] The use of ceramic floor tiles was also observed at house 'E' on Derngate and the excavator of St James' End suggested that the lack of pottery from 'floor' deposits may indicate the use of floorboards in the late medieval period – a trend that has been identified in Coventry from the presence of joist marks.[60] In the backyards of many houses, proper metalled surfaces also began to be laid down during this period, while the use of ceramic or stone roof tiles became much more common during the later middle ages.[61]

Although artefacts can be an indicator of status, it is rare to find items that prove the occupiers of a site were wealthy. Exceptions to this are found at 'The Riding', where fragments of drinking glasses and two fine knives were found in early sixteenth-century contexts, and at the 'Guildhall Extension', where a fragment of medieval decorated window-glass was discovered.[62] The finds at The Riding confirm that this was a very high status site, which makes sense given that the east part of the town was occupied by gentry families and the excavation took place on a piece of land that was formerly part of Gobion Manor. The discovery of the

---

58 Williams, *St Peter's Street*, 20, 31, 42, 87.

59 Williams and Farewell, 'Excavations in The Riding', 104.

60 Shaw, 'Medieval site at Derngate', 75; Shaw and Soden, *Travis Perkins site St James' End.*

61 At St Peter's, ceramic and stone roof tiles make an appearance from c.1250, but the great majority came from fifteenth-century contexts. Williams, *St Peter's Street*, 325, 327.

62 Williams and Farewell 'The Riding', 92; Shaw, 'Recent work in medieval Northampton: Archaeological excavations on St Giles' Street, 1990, and at St Edmund's End, 1988', 115.

decorated window glass at the Guildhall Extension is also unsurprising, given that this site was located in the commercial core of the late medieval town.

Within the town as a whole, one major change that could be interpreted as a sign of wealth is the increased use of road paving and metalling. The practice of surfacing the roads was not a new development in the later middle ages, for evidence of metalling accompanies the first formal laying out of streets in around the late eleventh-thirteenth centuries. For instance on St Peter's Street and Narrow Toe Lane the road appears to have received a metalled surface at the same time as the houses in the area became formally aligned along the street.[63] In some of the watching briefs around the town there is also evidence of what may have been twelfth to thirteenth-century road surfacing. For example at Sheep Street early road surfaces were identified and one of these had organic remains resting on it that included sherds of pottery of late-twelfth to fourteenth-century date.[64] Yet, where it has been possible to date surfaces, most of the evidence points to the first substantial surfaces being of a later date. At Bath Street a series of metalled surfaces were identified of which the earliest sealed pottery that was no earlier than the thirteenth century and at Newlands a series of road surfaces were identified overlying a pit containing pottery of late-thirteenth to fourteenth-century date.[65] On St Peter's Street and Narrow Toe Lane the first substantial surfaces were not laid down until the fourteenth or fifteenth centuries, these consisting of compact ironstone and gravel surfaces of 10-20 centimetres thickness.[66] This increased use

[63] Williams, *St Peter's Street.* The early street surface is most clearly identified in plan in fig. 45, p. 76.

[64] W.R.G. Moore, 'Archaeology in Northamptonshire 1973', *Northamptonshire Archaeology*, 9 (1974), 107.

[65] R. Hunter, M. McCarthy and J. Williams, 'Archaeology in Northamptonshire 1975', *Northamptonshire Archaeology*, 11 (1976), 198-9; RCHM, *Northampton*, 392.

[66] Williams, *St Peter's Street, Northampton.* The thickness of the fifteenth-century surface has been estimated on the basis of three sections: fig. 20, layer 869, p. 30; fig. 46, layer 31, p. 77; fig. 50, layer 63, p. 86.

of road surfacing would appear to indicate that urban wealth was holding up despite the population decline and it suggests that the town's concern to improve its roads, as reflected by the 1431 Paving Act, did result in real advances in this area. Another sign that the population of the town was perhaps becoming more, rather than less, wealthy in the late middle ages, is the apparent change in methods of rubbish disposal. In the post-conquest period, industrial or domestic rubbish was typically disposed of in back yard pits. This practice largely came to an end in the fourteenth-fifteenth century. The lack of late medieval rubbish pits has been noted and commented on in many parts of the town and, indeed, is a phenomenon common in late medieval English towns.[67] From this point in time the presence of reusable stone-lined garderobes has been noted in Northampton and other towns and, as rubbish pitting in yards declined, it became more common for backyards to be given proper metalled surfaces. For instance, on St Peter's Street it is clear that at least three of the fifteenth-century houses had proper metalled yards and more may have been observed if the late medieval backyards had not been removed by machine.[68] Since two of the yards were made up of compact pitched stone surfaces, there must have been a considerable investment in yard surfacing. A similar development in yard surfacing can also be noted at Marefair where a stone pavement was laid down in the fifteenth century.[69]

This decline in rubbish pit digging seems to be associated with a move from private rubbish disposal to communal disposal – with waste presumably being carted outside the town after initial storage in garderobes or ground-level lay-stalls. This must have resulted in towns becoming cleaner places and the change in disposal practice is the main reason why there is less build-up of stratigraphy in towns from the late medieval period. This development may be associated with a desire to

---

[67] It has become something of a commonplace for Northampton's excavators to comment on this, e.g. Shaw, 'Black Lion Hill', 123.

[68] Houses 1, 4, 8: Williams, *St Peters Street*, 20, 53, 78-9.

[69] Williams, 'Excavations at Marefair', 51-2.

reduce the miasmas that were believed to encourage disease.[70] It is possible though that the development may also be associated with a shift towards the construction of better quality and longer lasting housing in the late middle ages. Once this happened townspeople would have had to stop dumping refuse in their backyards because otherwise the ground-levels of their backyards would continue to rise over time and it would be increasingly difficult to prevent their houses from being inundated by run-off from their yards. Yet, whatever the cause, the development of communal rubbish disposal and indeed the surfacing of backyards could only have been possible if the inhabitants of the town had been able to afford it.

Urban Functions

The following section will consider the archaeological evidence for the functions of medieval Northampton. It will also consider whether the town's functions changed during the later middle ages. This section will examine the military, political, ecclesiastical, agrarian, industrial and commercial / service functions of the town.

In the twelfth-thirteenth century Northampton was a military base of considerable importance. Located in the centre of England and standing astride the principal north-south road in the country it was heavily contested during a number of rebellions.[71] Its military significance is illustrated by both documentary and archaeological evidence relating to the castle. A 1743 plan of the castle indicates

---

[70] In the case of London it has been argued that attempts to improve the sanitary condition of the city were a direct result of plague outbreaks: E.L. Sabine, 'Butchering in Mediaeval London', *Speculum*, 8 (1933), 348; E.L. Sabine, 'Street cleaning in Mediaeval London', *Speculum*, 12 (1937), 27-9. Concern over the damaging effects of miasmas was also a major justification given for the passing of parliamentary statutes in the fourteenth and fifteenth centuries that sought to force municipal authorities to clean up towns and relocate noisome trades, such as butchers and tanners, outside their walls: *Statutes of the Realm*, vol. II, 59, 527-8.

[71] Until the later middle ages the main route between London and the North East was by way of Dunstable, Stony Stratford, Northampton and Leicester – the route only shifting on to the line of the 'Great North Road' (A1) at Grantham: *vide infra*, 9, n.16.

that it covered a total of 15 acres, with each of the two baileys encompassing an area of 3.5 acres.[72] Excavations carried out in the 1960s and 1970s indicate that the inner bailey ditch was 27 metres wide and 9 metres deep, while the outer bailey ditch was c.14 metres wide by 5.5 metres deep.[73] Within the inner bailey, excavators uncovered two large buildings in the north-east corner. These were of twelfth to thirteenth-century date and were identified as a kitchen block and a domestic suite with an accompanying undercroft.[74] At the height of its development, the castle was clearly a major fortress, while building accounts indicate that until the late thirteenth century large sums of money were regularly spent on repairs and improvements to the main defences.[75] After this it began to be neglected. The two buildings in the inner bailey had gone out of use by the fourteenth century and were not subsequently replaced. One of these was clearly destroyed by a fire. This fire is presumably the one mentioned in a 1323 survey, which indicated that the walls, towers, gates and barbican, were in a poor state and stated the whole castle would cost over £1000 to repair.[76] It appears, however, that the only major repairs conducted were those on the great hall that was used for the holding of the Eyre of 1329-30. Subsequently the main use of the castle appears to have been as a gaol.[77] The failure to maintain the defences through the late middle ages is confirmed by nineteenth-century 'rescue' excavations, which concluded that the remaining walls and gates were mid-thirteenth century. This conclusion is

---

[72] RCHM, *Northampton*, 334.

[73] J.H. Williams and M. Shaw, 'Excavations in Chalk Lane, Northampton, 1975-1978', *Northamptonshire Archaeology*, 16 (1981), 106-7.

[74] RCHM, *Northampton*, 335.

[75] For instance in 1266 the King ordered that the wall on the west side of the castle should be repaired and that a palisade outside the castle should be repaired. In 1266/7 £200 was spent on repairs and in the 1280's a further £250 was spent: RCHM, *Northampton*, 333.

[76] *Calendar of Inquisitions Miscellaneous* (1307-1349), 149.

[77] *VCH, Northamptonshire,* vol. III, 34-5.

supported further by the 1976 excavations, which revealed that the outer bailey ditch had largely silted up by the sixteenth century.[78]

Apart from the defence offered by the castle, the town walls of Northampton clearly reflected and contributed to its military importance. As late as 1278 it appears that they were in good condition, for an inquisition of that date noted that burgesses sometimes walked along one section of it in winter to avoid the muddy streets and it was said that the night watchmen patrolled it and spied from its battlements to observe malefactors entering or leaving the town.[79] After this time it is uncertain how well the wall was maintained. In 1300 the town received a five-year murage grant to repair the walls and in 1378 a commission was sent to the mayor and bailiffs ordering them 'to repair the walls, turrets, dykes and other defences of the town with all speed.'[80] Whether this was done is uncertain but in 1400 they received another murage grant of two years.[81] In 1549 the Privy Council ordered that stone should be taken from the steeple of St Edmunds 'for reparacion of their towne walles and west bridge there' but this would only have allowed for minor repairs considering that the wall encompassed an area of 245 acres.[82] It is at least clear that by the seventeenth century the walls were in very poor repair, for a Civil War surveyor described them as 'miserably ruined'.[83]

Since it is uncertain from the documentary evidence whether the walls were maintained in a militarily fit state, their condition provides an obvious subject for archaeological enquiry. Unfortunately most excavations that have attempted to

---

[78] E.F. Law, 'The Ruins at the Old Castle, Northampton', *Associated Architectural Societies Reports and Papers*, 15 (1873), 201; Williams and Shaw 'Excavations in Chalk Lane', 105-8.

[79] *VCH, Northamptonshire*, vol. III, 30.

[80] *Calendar of Patent Rolls* (1377-81), 273.

[81] *Calendar of Patent Rolls* (1399-1400), 361.

[82] *Acts of the Privy Council* (1547-1550), 391.

[83] *Calendar of State Papers, Domestic* (1641-43), 385.

assess their development have been inconclusive. At the 'Mounts', an excavation in 1973 uncovered the foundations of what were possibly two phases of wall building, the second dating to between 1100 and 1400.[84] A ditch appeared to be associated with this but was only 2 metres deep by 2-3 metres wide. This had been allowed to silt up and a recut, made sometime between 1250-1500, was only 1.5 metres deep by 1.5 metres wide. If this was the town ditch, it would clearly have been of limited military utility. Another excavation, at George Street, identified a ditch of c.4 metres wide by 2 metres deep, but failed to identify an associated wall. Fortunately, the excavation in 1995 of a site just south of the west gate has proved more successful.[85] This uncovered a series of defences on the western edge of the town. The earliest defences were a Saxon bank and ditch, but improvements were carried out in the twelfth century when the ditch was widened and a two-metre thick stone wall was built on top of the bank. By the middle of the seventeenth century the ditch had almost entirely silted up and it is unclear how much of the wall survived by that time. Although two new ditches were cut during the Civil War, by the late seventeenth century these had been completely filled in and what was left of the wall was levelled. Although this is little to go on, the evidence relating to the upkeep of town walls, combined with the better evidence from the castle, suggests that by the late middle ages the town had ceased to be a centre of great military significance or potential.

Apart from being an important military centre in the twelfth-thirteenth centuries, Northampton was often a focus point for nationally important political events. These included the holding of a number of parliaments and the use of the town as a rallying point for the Crusades. The town's role on the national stage declined, however, in the fourteenth century; the last parliament held there was in 1380 and

---

84 J.H. Williams, 'Four small excavations on Northampton's medieval defences and elsewhere', *Northamptonshire Archaeology*, 17 (1982), 63-5.

85 Shaw, Chapman and Soden, 'Northampton', 409-11.

after that time it rarely featured as a focus for national political activity. The town nevertheless remained an important centre for county politics and, indeed, the decline of royal influence may have increased opportunities for Northamptonshire's gentry to compete for power and influence over both the town and county. It is certainly the case that the gentry maintained impressive houses in the eastern quarter of the town, which, in the case of The Riding site, can be shown to date back to the late middle ages. The impressive late medieval Council House (illustrated on the front cover) would also seem to reflect the importance of political action and expression within the town.

Northampton was a significant ecclesiastical centre in the middle ages. The important priory of St Andrew's lay at the north end of the town, St James' Abbey lay a mile to the west, a nunnery lay to the south at Delapre and all four orders of friars maintained houses within the town. There were also four hospitals and a college in or very close to the town. Together all these houses probably occupied about a quarter of the town's space. Archaeological investigation of the religious houses has shown that all the sites investigated appear to have continued to be developed in the fifteenth century, which indicates that Northampton remained a focus for ecclesiastical activity throughout the late middle ages.

Agrarian activity in the town is less well attested than at Leicester. Although 'cultivation' soils of late medieval date have been noted at St Peter's Street and Swan Street, the only clear evidence of horticultural activity is that found at Swan Street – where bedding trenches associated with fragments of watering pots were found. These cultivation features dated to 1500-1650.[86] It seems likely that many of the unoccupied areas of the town were being used at this time for intensive forms of horticulture such as orchards or market gardening. Although there is not much archaeological evidence of horticultural / agricultural activity, the Borough

---

[86] Shaw and Steadman, 'Swan Street, Northampton', 137, 154.

Records make constant reference to the town's meadows, pastures and the animals kept there. For instance, an ordinance of 1553 proclaimed that no freeman of the town should 'keep moor for his franchis than iii bestes upon the commons in alle, and that they be his owne'.[87]

Most of the evidence for industrial activity from the town comes from the western quarter. At Marefair, iron-forging slag, a blacksmith's punch, lead sheet offcuts and copper alloy sheet fragments were found in the yard of the twelfth to fourteenth-century building.[88] Similar evidence of metalworking was found in the property's fifteenth-century yard, suggesting continuity in the function of this site. At House 4 on St Peter's Street there was also evidence of late medieval metalworking with waste materials indicating that pins and lace tags were made there.[89] An artefact that was interpreted as a fifteenth-century button sheet was also found there, although this may in fact be a belt plate.

A number of grain-drying ovens have been identified at Northampton. At St Peter's Street two of these were built in the yard of House 10 in the early fifteenth century and drying ovens of fourteenth to fifteenth-century date were also identified to the south at the Green.[90] These were filled in when both areas were converted to tanneries in the later fifteenth century. At Marefair an oven was constructed in the yard in the late fourteenth-fifteenth century. It too contained various grains and has been interpreted as a grain-drying oven.[91] Since grain-drying tends to be particularly associated with malting, it is possible that during the late fourteenth-fifteenth century there was a particular focus in at least the preparatory stages of ale making in the western part of the town. It seems likely

---

[87] *VCH, Northamptonshire,* vol. III, 22-3.

[88] Williams, 'Excavations at Marefair', 52-4.

[89] Williams, *St Peter's Street*, 145, 260-3.

[90] Williams, *St Peter's Street*, 96-7, Shaw, 'The Green', 72.

[91] Williams, 'Excavations at Marefair', 52.

that this industry was driven out by the growth of the tanning industry in that area. Since tanning is a particularly noxious industry and the fumes caused by it might have affected the taste of the grain, the malters could have had good reason to relocate. Apart from these drying ovens, two other ovens of uncertain function were identified at the top of Swan Street.[92] These were of thirteenth to fourteenth-century date. It has been suggested that the large number of hearths in the late medieval house fronting on to St Peter's Street at Black Lion Hill indicate that this house was a bakery.[93] It too was abandoned around the time that the tanning industry became predominant in the western part of the town.

Whatever the precise range of industrial occupations in the western part of the town during the fourteenth-fifteenth centuries, it is clear that some time around the late fifteenth century the area was taken over by tanners. At House 10, St Peter's Street, a tanning pit of c.1470 has been identified and immediately to the south, on The Green, a tanning complex was constructed around 1470-1550.[94] On the north side of St Peter's Street it appears that House 4 was also being used for some activity associated with tanning or leather working after 1470, for pits dug through the back yard contain large numbers of horn cores and horse bones, which are typical tanners' waste. In one of these pits metal tools that could be associated with leather working were also found.[95] To the west of St Peter's Street, at Black Lion Hill, a late medieval cat skeleton was found that showed evidence of skinning – again suggesting the use of the area for processing animal skins.[96] In the sixteenth century the evidence for tanning activity in this area is even more overwhelming, with at least three major tanning complexes of c. 1550 date having been identified

---

[92] Shaw, 'Derngate', 66, 69.

[93] Shaw, 'Black Lion Hill', 121-3.

[94] Shaw, 'The Green', 72-85.

[95] Williams, *St Peter's Street*, 55-6, 189-90, 268, 271-3 328-9.

[96] Shaw, 'Excavations on a Saxon and Medieval Site at Black Lion Hill', 123.

at St Peter's Street and The Green.[97] Since there is no evidence of domestic occupation in the area after c.1500 it seems possible that the tanneries may have driven out domestic occupation from the area after this time. Tanneries remained a prominent industry in this part of the town into the modern period.

Commercial and service activities clearly constituted important functions of the late medieval town, but these are little attested in the archaeological record. One exception to this is the identification of what was almost certainly a medieval inn at 34 Gold Street, in the centre of the medieval town. This consisted of a substantial property with an entrance alleyway leading to a building arranged around a courtyard. This is a typical layout for a medieval or early modern inn and the property was certainly known as 'Goat Inn' from the sixteenth to seventeenth century. In the courtyard a number of wells were examined during rescue excavations in 1970. Finds from these included three whole decorated medieval jugs of thirteenth to fifteenth-century date.[98] At Causeway Lane, Leicester, it was noted that assemblages dominated by jugs are typical of inns.[99] Since the dropping of whole jugs down wells would certainly seem to be an activity more likely to be associated with an inn than a domestic household, it does seem highly probable that this site was also an inn during the later middle ages. This constitutes very limited evidence of service activities but the importance of commerce and services to the town can at least be detected in the general topographical development of the town.

As noted earlier, during the fourteenth-fifteenth centuries, the population of the town contracted and some back-street areas such as Swan Street and Fetter Lane were abandoned. Yet the commercial centre of the town along the main north-

---

[97] Williams, *St Peter's Street*, 98-103; Shaw, 'The Green', 72-85.

[98] M.R. McCarthy, 'Medieval finds from Gold Street, Northampton', *Northamptonshire Archaeology*, 12 (1977), 196-8.

[99] A. Connor and R. Buckley, *Roman and Medieval Occupation in Causeway Lane, Leicester* (Leicester Archaeological Monographs, No. 5, 1999), p. 86.

south streets of the Drapery / Bridge Street / College Street and also east-west streets of Gold Street and Derngate, appear to have remained prosperous. The building of fourteenth-century cellars south of All Saints Church and on College Street and the Drapery, together with the continued intense development of the back of the property at Guildhall Extension, points to a high demand for property in the centre of the town. Similar developments were noted at Leicester and Stamford where, despite the overall contraction in population, there appears to have been an intensification of occupation along the main commercial streets and around the markets, characterised by the expansion of houses into the backs of their tenement blocks and the building of third storeys on the front ranges. The large inn identified on Gold Street indicates the importance of servicing visiting or passing travellers, while the very prosperity of the medieval All Saints Church, reported by early modern commentators to be the finest in Northampton, might suggest that the commercial core of the town remained prosperous. It is thus clear that while commerce has left few artefactual markers, the activity still had a profound influence on the nature and form of the Northampton's development.

Artefact Networks and the Urban Hierarchy

If mid-sized county towns such as Northampton, Stamford and Leicester were articulators of regional commerce and marketing, it may be expected that their specialised roles might be detectable in the archaeological record. In particular, it might be expected that their central role in marketing would result in a broader range of artefact types from a greater geographical spread being found in them. The best evidence of the geographical diversity of artefact types is almost inevitably going to be that associated with ceramics, but for meaningful discussions of this to be possible, large assemblages that have been thoroughly analysed by ceramics experts are necessary. At the St Peters Street excavations such analysis was conducted. It revealed that local wares dominated the medieval pottery assemblage. In the period 1100-c.1400 the most common type was the Olney /

Lyveden ware (T2), but by the fifteenth century this was supplanted by Potterspury type ware (W18), covering the period 1250-1500. Nevertheless, throughout the middle ages a trickle of regional imports was noted to a greater extent than would be expected on rural sites. Pottery types included wares from Brill and Warwickshire and decorated jugs from London and Nottingham.[100] The presence of such regional imports may also be noted at Black Lion Hill. Of the 894 sherds from phase 4Aii (1350-1500), 65 came from Brill (W14) and 10 were of East Anglian Red Ware (W15).[101] Apart from such large assemblages, small groups of ceramics do sometimes throw light on the extent of the town's contacts. Perhaps the best example of this is The Riding where eight fragments of later medieval Dutch floor tiles were found. This is an exceptional group of a type which would not be expected in a village or even in a small town. It is worth noting, however, that even on the wealthy Riding site in a large county town like Northampton, most of the medieval pottery was of local types, with just a few regional imports such as Brill and Oxfordshire ware.[102] This probably reflects the fact that pottery is not a very sensitive status indicator in this period, for wealthy people were likely to represent their status, not by buying expensive imported pottery, but by replacing pottery with metal goods, such as pewter or silver.

Conclusion

The archaeological evidence suggests that Northampton experienced a radical population decline during the late middle ages. A number of excavations on the periphery of the medieval town, including those at Kettering Road, St John's Street, Swan street and Victoria Promenade, indicate that land occupied by houses in the thirteenth century was given over to horticulture in the fourteenth-fifteenth

[100] Williams, *St Peter's Street,* 228-9.

[101] Shaw, 'Black Lion Hill', 124.

[102] Williams and Farwell, 'The Riding', 97, 104.

centuries. At other sites, such as St James' End, Black Lion Hill and Woolmonger Street, the intensity of occupation also appears to have declined in this period. The failure to expand the parochial space of those parish churches which have survived to the modern day suggests that the number of people living in their parishes did not grow. Nevertheless, there is no evidence that the central core of the town became depopulated in the later middle ages. During the fourteenth century cellared buildings were constructed on George Row, the Drapery and the south end of College Street and a substantial two-storeyed stone building existed on the Guildhall Extension site, just to the east of All Saints. This suggests that there was still competition for land in the middle of the town, even after the population decline had begun. Substantial properties were also developed at Derngate and The Riding at this time.

Apart from the general contraction of the town, there is some evidence of an increase in geographical specialisation within Northampton during the fifteenth to sixteenth centuries. The west end of the town, in the vicinity of St Peter's, changed from a mixed domestic-industrial area in the fourteenth-fifteenth century into an entirely industrial zone specialising in tanning by the late fifteenth-sixteenth century. By contrast, the area around the market place was a wealthy and intensely developed commercial area, containing inns and fine stone houses. The eastern side of the town also had some very wealthy properties in it. It seems likely that the one excavated at The Riding belonged to a gentry family, and this part of the town may well have developed into something of a gentry quarter during the late medieval period.

Although population decline almost certainly caused the town's economy to shrink in absolute terms, the per-capita incomes of the remaining inhabitants probably rose during the later fourteenth to early fifteenth centuries. Domestic properties ranged from the fine buildings noted at Gobion Manor, Guildhall Extension and Derngate, to the poorer, but still respectable tenements, constructed along St Peter's

Street in the fifteenth century. By this period the sort of semi-sunken urban hovels of thirteenth-century Swan Street had disappeared, which probably reflects the improved circumstances of the poorer sort during the late middle ages – as depopulation forced down rents and pushed up wages. The wealth of the remaining inhabitants is also reflected in the higher quality of their ceramic wares, their construction of an impressive new council house and the peoples' continued ability to both beautify their parish churches and support the development of friaries and hospitals within the town. Lastly, money also appears to have been directed into improving the town's urban environment during the late middle ages, probably because miasmas (bad smells) were believed to cause disease. As a result, the roads were better paved, waste appears to have been carted out of the town (rather than being buried in back-yard pits) and noxious industries, such as tanneries, seem to have been segregated from the centres of population. So, while the town was undoubtedly smaller in the late middle ages, it was probably a rather pleasanter and more attractive place in which to live.

During the late medieval period Northampton ceased, along with most other towns in central England, to be an important military centre. Both the castle and the walls fell into disrepair and insofar as its defences were maintained this was probably only done to preserve a sense of civic identity and provide the municipality with a mechanism for controlling commerce. At this time Northampton ceased to act as a centre for national political events, such as the holding of parliament. This does not mean though that the local gentry ceased to use it as a focal point for their activities, or that it stopped being the commercial and industrial centre for its county. The continued importance of commerce is most clearly reflected in the fairly intense development of properties close to the junction of the main roads and the market place. While the archaeological materials found in Northampton suggest that most of its trade was conducted with its local hinterland, the identification of ceramic goods from Oxfordshire, East Anglia and even the Low Countries indicates that it was also tied in to longer distance commercial networks.

As for industry, it is apparent that, while the town's cloth industry may have been in decline, large-scale tanneries were being developed in the western part of the town by end of the fifteenth century. This expansion of the tanning industry was an important development for the town, since it laid the foundations for the town's early modern success as England's leading boot and shoe manufacturing centre.

The foregoing study, based on the archaeological evidence from the town, has revealed a great deal about how the town developed as a physical, topographic and economic entity during the late middle ages. It has suggested that while Northampton shrank in absolute size and became a less politically important place, it was able to maintain a position as a significant, and probably more pleasant, county town, capable of servicing the commercial, industrial and cultural needs of Northamptonshire. Archaeology is, however, but one means by which Northampton's medieval past can be investigated. Despite the destruction of many documents through accident or neglect, many valuable records survive in Northamptonshire Record Office, the Public Record Office and private archives. While such records rarely grab the public's attention in the way that a new excavation does, they contain a treasure trove of often-neglected information. The following study, by Dr. Jane Laughton, will use these records to examine the issues discussed in the archaeological section of the paper. By doing this it will be possible to learn much more about late medieval Northampton and it will reveal the extent to which archaeological and documentary research can complement each other when conducted together.

THE DOCUMENTARY EVIDENCE

Jane Laughton

The documentary sources which are available for Northampton have particular strengths and weaknesses. The borough records are disappointing, and consist largely of a compilation of rules and legal precedents known as the *Liber Custumarum Villae Norhamptoniae* begun in c.1460, with subsequent rules and decisions added at later dates.[103] There are no borough court rolls. The account of money from fines and amercements levied by a court sometime in the reign of Edward I appears to be one of the few surviving judicial records.[104] The taxation records are far from comprehensive. Details of the subsidy assessment of 1301, for example, can be found only for the *vicus* of St James.[105] There are no nominative lists for the subsidies of 1327 and 1333, and merely a small section of what purports to be a nominative list of poll-tax payers in 1381.[106] Two lists of those who contributed to the subsidies in 1524 and in 1525 do exist, however, and their value is enhanced by the fact that the occupations of most of the tax payers were also recorded.[107] Estreat rolls dating from 1520-1 and relating to two of the town's wards (Chequer Ward and the East Quarter) provide contemporary evidence.[108]

Among the most useful sources for the study of late medieval Northampton is a detailed rental dating from the reign of Edward I that recorded contributions to the

---

103 *NBR*, vol. I, 197-430.

104 'Profits of the Court of Northampton *temp.* Ed I', *Northamptonshire Notes and Queries*, new series, 5 (1921-3), 203-11.

105 PRO, E 179/155/31, mm. 3, 4.

106 PRO, E 179/155/41, m. 1.

107 PRO, E 179/155/124; E 179/155/138. See A. Dyer, 'Northampton in 1524', *Northamptonshire Past and Present*, 6 (1979), 73-80. There are one or two discrepancies between the figures quoted there and those used in this paper.

108 NRO, Royal Charters 30, 31.

farm of the town street by street.[109] This can be compared with the rental listing the same properties which was newly drawn up in 1503-4.[110] Other topographical information is provided by a rental of St James' Abbey dating from 1332, by some private charters and leases, and by the grants and leases printed in the *Catalogue of Ancient Deeds*.[111] A memoranda roll of 1378-9 recorded some property transactions, and also a list of mayoral receipts.[112] A list of purveyances by the royal household at Northampton in 1301 survives.[113] The most rewarding documentary source, however, has undoubtedly been the will register for the archdeaconry of Northampton, which contains copies of the wills made by some 142 townspeople and registered in the years 1462-1510.[114] The value of such records to the study of late medieval towns will be readily apparent in the following discussion.

The historical section of this working paper does not attempt to provide a comprehensive study of Northampton in the late medieval period but will focus on the subjects and issues raised in the foregoing archaeological study. The research project was an interdisciplinary undertaking, concerned to bring together the documentary and the material evidence. Both types of evidence existed for Northampton in some quantity, and it is hoped that the collation and comparison of both sources will illustrate the problems and possibilities of this interdisciplinary

---

[109] PRO, SC 12/13/38.

[110] NRO, Royal Charter 29. John Williams has transcribed the two rentals and hopes to publish them.

[111] BL, Add. Ch. 6117; NRO, Private Charters (listed in Northamptonshire Borough Records, Box 41).

[112] NRO, Royal Charter 28.

[113] BL, Add. Ch. 75994.

[114] Early Will Register. Although the official NRO title for this collection is currently 'Northampton Early Wills, 1467-1510' the earliest will dates from 1462. A group of volunteers is in the process of transcribing the wills, under the guidance of Jacky Minchington.

approach. To facilitate comparison between the two sets of data, topics will be considered in the sequence adopted in the archaeological section.

Parish churches

Discussion of the parish churches is largely based upon the evidence of wills and thus deals with the situation as it was in the second half of the fifteenth century and early sixteenth century. Northampton had nine parish churches, all established by 1130: All Saints', St Giles', St Michael's, Holy Sepulchre, St Mary's (by the Castle), St Gregory's, St Peter's, St Edmund's and St Bartholomew's. The exact location of the parish boundaries is not certain but it seems that the first seven churches served the intra-mural area, with St Edmund's providing for the eastern suburb and St Bartholomew's for the northern suburb. During the thirteenth century St Leonard's Hospital appears to have assumed parochial functions for the southern suburb, while St Margaret's assumed similar rights for the western suburb.[115] These developments may be indicative of the growth of these suburbs in that period.

An idea of the relative wealth of the parishes in 1428 is given by the taxation figures in the Feudal Aids: St Peter's (£26 13s 4d), All Saints' (£13 6s 8d), St Giles' (£4 13s 4d), Holy Sepulchre (£2 13s 4d), St Gregory's (£2 12s 0d), St Mary's (£2), St Michael's (£2), St Edmund's (£1). The figure for St Peter's is inflated by the inclusion of income drawn from its dependent chapelries of Kingsthorpe and Upton. In the *Valor Ecclesiasticus* of 1535 St Peter's again headed the list (£41 6s 8d), followed by All Saints' (£16), St Giles' (£8), Holy

---

[115] RCHM, *Northampton*, 53-4. It is suggested here that a major period of church foundation in Northampton coincided with the great post-Conquest economic expansion of the town. Compare Lincoln (35 parishes by 1100), York (over 40 by 1200), and the medieval parishes of Norwich (c.60), London (over 100), Canterbury (22), Oxford (17), Cambridge and Stamford (14 each): figures taken from Williams, *Saxon and Medieval Northampton*, 46-7.

Sepulchre (just over £6), St Mary's (£2 13s 4d), St Gregory's (£2 13s 4d), St Edmund's (18s 2d) and St Michael's (16s 7d).[116] These figures suggest that All Saints' was by far the wealthiest of Northampton's parish churches in the late medieval period. The position of St Peter's must remain uncertain. St Bartholomew's had apparently lost its parochial status some time after 1232. It does not appear in the Feudal Aid of 1428 and the dedication seems to have been changed to St Lawrence either in the late fifteenth or early sixteenth century. Later in the sixteenth century St Edmund's (c.1540), St Michael's, St Gregory's (1556) and St Mary's (1590) also lost their parochial status.[117]

The respective rankings of the parish churches are to some extent reflected in the wills. Ninety-three of the 142 wills in the Early Register were made by testators who requested burial in the church of All Saints' or in its churchyard. Fifteen testators were parishioners of St Giles', and nine were parishioners of St Peter's. St Gregory's was specified as the place of burial by five testators, Holy Sepulchre and St Mary's by three, while the church of St Michael's was named in two wills. The churches of St Edmund's and of St Leonard's were each named once. It should be noted that three townspeople requested burial in the church of St John's Hospital and two others asked to be buried in St James' Abbey. St Andrew's monastery, the abbey of St Mary de la Pre, and the chapel of St Katherine were each named once. Thirty-nine of the 59 Northampton wills proved in the Prerogative Court of Canterbury before 1520 were made by townspeople connected with All Saints'

[116] Williams, *Saxon and Medieval Northampton*, 47 (where the figures are given as percentages).

[117] RCHM, *Northampton*, 56. It should be noted that the chapel of St Bartholomew is mentioned in a will of 1490: R.M. Serjeantson and H.I. Longden, 'The Parish Churches and Religious Houses of Northamptonshire: their dedications, altars, images and lights', *Archaeological Journal*, 70 (1913), 379.

Church, compared to St Giles' (9), Holy Sepulchre (4), St Mary's and St Gregory's (2 each), and one apiece for St Margaret's, St James' and the Black Friars.[118]

These figures are not indicators of the size of parochial populations, firstly, because only the wealthier members of the community made wills, and secondly, because the wills themselves reveal that All Saints' Church was sometimes specified as the chosen place of burial by testators who did not live within the parish.[119] These townspeople were doubtless influenced by the particular role that this church played in civic life and by the fact that All Saints' housed several of Northampton's most prestigious guilds. In Leicester St Martin's Church enjoyed a parallel pre-eminence deriving from similar functions. Indeed, it seems possible that the presence of a 'civic' church closely linked to members of the governing elite may itself be interpreted as a defining feature of a top-ranking town.

All Saints' Church – This church, first mentioned in 1108, stood to the south of the market place, at the heart of the medieval town. Its position as 'town' church was indicated (for example) by the fact that mass was celebrated here before the elections of town officials under the Act of 1489, and by the presence of special seats assigned to the mayor and bailiffs both before and after the fire of 1675.[120] It was the ringing of the 'great and more solemn' bell of All Saints' at 9 p.m. each night that signalled the curfew; no-one was to go without lights in the streets after

---

[118] *Prerogative Court of Canterbury Wills, 1383-1558* (Index Library; British Record Society, x and xi, 1893-5), *passim.*

[119] E.g., by William Mylle in 1492 (Early Will Register, f. 95r), by Robert Mese in 1494 (*ibid.*, f. 102r), and by Nicholas Bowker in 1498 (*ibid.*, f. 117r); all three men lived outside the South Gate. Henry Caysho, mayor of Northampton in 1424-5, lived in Swinewell Street, but was buried in the Corpus Christi chapel in All Saints', where his will was proved in May 1435 (BL, Add. Ch. 735).

[120] *VCH, Northamptonshire,* vol. III, 9, 56. For a description of the church as it was before the fire, see the comments of Henry Lee, town clerk in 1675, who quoted a saying that it had been 'as large as some cathedrals' (*ibid.*, 48-9).

this without reasonable excuse.[121] At some point before 1530 the 'clock house' was built over the chapel of St John the Baptist.[122]

Seven fraternities had altars and/or chapels in All Saints' Church in the later medieval period: the guilds of Corpus Christi, of St John the Baptist, of St Mary, of Holy Trinity and the Blessed Virgin Mary, of the Rood, of St George and of St Osyth. Of these, the guilds of Corpus Christi and of St Mary appear to have been the most prestigious, with members drawn from the ruling elite. In 1459-60 a foundation charter was granted to the college of All Saints, which had been founded by the vicar for himself and for the guild chaplains, who numbered sixteen or more.[123] At about the same time a fraternity of St Katherine was founded to assist burial of those who had died of the plague; a chapel was built for mortuary purposes and a burial ground provided (between College Lane and Horsemarket). This removed the dangers arising from burials of plague victims in the churchyard of All Saints', which was sited in the heart of the town. At the Dissolution the townsmen maintained that the chapel and churchyard of St Katherine had existed 'time out of mind' to safeguard the health of inhabitants and visitors. They also claimed that the shoemakers of the town resorted to the chapel and each gave 12d for the priest, and that repairs were paid for by the mayor, burgesses and shoemakers.[124]

The creation of this chapel and graveyard underlines the central location of the church of All Saints'. References in property deeds also indicate how closely linked the church was with the commercial hub of the town. In 1358, for example,

---

[121] *NBR*, vol. I, 252.

[122] Serjeantson and Longden, 'Parish churches of Northamptonshire', 372-3.

[123] R.M. Serjeantson, *History of the Church of All Saints', Northampton* (Northampton, 1901), 67-72. The college, which allowed the chaplains to live together under a definite rule, had been in existence for some years on a less formal basis (RCHM, *Northampton*, 56).

[124] Serjeantson, *History of All Saints*, 60-1.

a capital messuage with adjacent shops was described as lying opposite the churchyard and church of All Saints'; the rental of 1503-4 listed rents from six shops described as 'opposite the west gable of All Saints'.[125] Its centrality was also emphasised by one of the aims of the guild of St Mary, cited in the guild certificate of 1389. The fraternity had been founded 'time without memory', and among the aims was that of providing visitors and others whose business took them from the town with an opportunity to hear mass. A choral service, with organ accompaniment, was provided daily at sunset; this usually attracted a large congregation.[126]

A number of Northampton's craft guilds were associated with the church. In 1452 it was ordained that half the fines imposed on the town's fullers were to be used to maintain three tapers at the altar of St John the Baptist. In 1467 the ordinances for the fishmongers laid down that fish sold upon 'bakstalles' was to be forfeited, with half the profits going to the maintenance of lights in 'the high place afore the Rode' in All Saints', which had long been maintained by people selling fish. A memorandum of 1494, agreed in the presence of the mayor and recorder in the chapel of Corpus Christi, decreed that no bakers were to keep any manner of 'ostery' which could receive more than four horses, and that no innholders were to bake horse-bread or man's bread. And in 1511 the weavers' ordinances stipulated that half the fines incurred by these craftsmen were to go to the fraternity of the Trinity.[127] In 1490 the innholder Hugo Wodfall left 3s 4d to the light called the 'Bowers lyght' hanging before the little cross.[128]

---

[125] *Catalogue of Ancient Deeds*, vol. IV, A 8107; NRO, Royal Charter 29.

[126] Serjeantson, *History of All Saints*, 45-7; H.F. Westlake, *The Parish Gilds of Medieval England* (London, 1919), Appendix: The Gild Certificates of 1389, no. 383.

[127] *NBR*, vol. I, 292, 307-8, 331, 358. The fishmongers' ordinances noted that this devotion was being withdrawn because the customary places were no longer being used.

[128] Early Will Register, f. 92r.

The wills provide some information of the interior of the church in the medieval period. The chapel of St George and the altar of St Osyth were located in the south aisle; a light burned before the Five Wounds in the middle aisle; the sacrament light was to be found in the high choir; the fraternity of the Rood focused in the place where St Guthlac's picture was to be found.[129] The most prestigious burials took place within the guild chapels, particularly the chapels of Corpus Christi and of the Blessed Virgin Mary. In 1434 the former mayor Henry Caysho asked to be buried in the chapel of Corpus Christi, next to the marble stone of a fellow mercer; in 1500 William Perwyn, perhaps the bailiff of 1494, asked to be buried next to his seat in the chapel of Corpus Christi, and directed his wife to provide a stone costing £5 for his tomb. Images of himself and of his wife were to be carved upon this stone, together with images of their children – ten sons on the father's side and seven girls on the side of the mother.[130] The wills also indicate something of the appearance of the churchyard. It seems that failing burial within the church, then a grave next to the exterior wall of one of the chapels was the most sought-after location.[131] Other testators asked to be buried to the north of the church next to the processional way, in the churchyard next to the great oak, or against the wedding door.[132] Such documentary evidence is particularly valuable when, as is the case with All Saints', the church itself has been destroyed.

It should be emphasised that it would be misleading to interpret the size and splendour of this church as an unambiguous indicator of population growth in this parish. All Saints' fulfilled a particular role within the community and became the focus for the devotions of men and women who lived in other parts of the town. The ruling elite and the members of the most prestigious fraternities (often the

---

[129] Serjeantson and Longden, 'Parish churches of Northamptonshire', 371-6.

[130] BL Add. Ch. 735; Early Will Register, f. 81v. For other examples of elite burials, see ff. 86r, 97v.

[131] E.g., Early Will Register, ff. 46v, 82r.

[132] Early Will Register, ff. 48v, 100v, 135r.

same men) were drawn to the church in the market place and it benefited from their legacies. Conversely, their largesse may have been to the detriment of other parish churches, which perhaps seemed poorer as a result.

St Peter's Church – The surviving structural remains of this church suggest an origin linked with the castle, for which indeed it may have served as a royal free chapel. By the late medieval period, however, the castle had declined in importance, and any particular association with St Peter's had apparently been lost. The nine surviving wills indicate that the church was a typical parish church fulfilling the usual parochial functions.[133] Bequests were made to the high altar and to altars dedicated to St John, to St Nicholas, to St Michael, to St Katherine, to the Blessed Virgin (whose altar stood in a separate chapel), and to the fraternity of St 'Rigiver' (St Ragenor) which was based in the church. One request for burial in the chancel survives; other parishioners were buried in the churchyard, with the area before the christening door perhaps a prime location. The sole reference to burial within the church suggests that most parishioners could not afford this distinction.

The occupations of the testators indicate that St Peter's served an area of the town inhabited by craftsmen rather than by retailers and merchants. Among them were several tanners, a fuller and a weaver; their occupations will be discussed in more detail below. Named as witnesses were butchers, shoemakers, weavers, dyers and tanners. Bequests included woollen cloth, money for wax tapers acquired from the sale of sheep and lambs, and rents from tenements in 'le Barkers end' within the parish. In 1496 the chandler John Essex, who was himself buried in the chapel of Corpus Christi in All Saints', left rent from a fish stall in the market to be used to maintain the fishers' light in the church of St Peter's, a bequest confirmed by his

[133] Early Will Register, ff. 16v, 18r, 23r, 48r, 92v, 123v, 129v, 147r, 158v .

widow in 1503.[134] The wills attested links between men who shared the same craft, and also family relationships.[135] St Peter's parish appears to have been a close-knit community, with a particular 'industrial' ambience deriving from tanning activities.

St Giles' Church – The figures from the Feudal Aid of 1428 and from the *Valor Ecclesiasticus* of 1535 suggest that among the parish churches of Northampton in the later medieval period the church of St Giles ranked second in wealth.[136] This position is echoed in the number of surviving wills. Fifteen wills made by testators of this parish are recorded in the Register, a figure (greatly) surpassed only by the wills for All Saints'.[137] Mention is made of chapels of the Blessed Virgin Mary and of St Peter, each with a picture of the patron saint; the chapel of Our Lady also contained a picture of St Katherine. St Peter's chapel was located on the south side of the church; a coffer stood beside the altar. There were altars dedicated to St George and to St James, and a fraternity dedicated to St Clement. Wills of the early sixteenth century mentioned an altar of St Nicholas and a guild of the Holy Cross.[138]

Testators included a wiredrawer, a grazier, a cooper, a carpenter and a shearman, but the striking feature of the parish is that it was distinguished by a marked

---

[134] Early Will Register, ff. 111v-112r, 158r. This reference to the fishers' light being in St Peter's Church by 1496 indicates that the complaint made in 1467 that the lights before the Rood in All Saints' were no longer being maintained by the fishmongers had some foundation (*NBR*, vol. I, 307-8).

[135] In 1475 the will of the tanner Rad West was witnessed by two tanners, one of them William Harpole; a third tanner acted as supervisor. In 1487 the sister of William Harpole left a brass pot to her goddaughter Alice Harpole, and a silver spoon to her godson William West. (Early Will Register, ff. 16v, 123v-124r).

[136] It should be remembered that the wealth of St Peter's Church cannot be determined, since the figure was inflated by the inclusion of income from the dependent chapelries of Kingsthorpe and Upton.

[137] Early Will Register, ff. 13r, 19v, 22v, 24r (2 wills), 25r, 39r, 42v, 52r, 75v, 90r, 133r, 134r, 148v, 165r.

[138] Serjeantson and Longden, 'Parish churches of Northamptonshire', 377-8.

'gentry' presence. The two men described as *armiger* in the Will Register were buried in chapels in St Giles' Church, and although Thomas Harowden esquire was content with burial 'where God provides', his bequest to the high altar in the church indicated that this was his parish; his widow is attested living there a few months later.[139] Indeed, only William Austyn gentleman is known to have been buried in another of Northampton's parish churches. In his will (6 September 1488) Austyn specified burial in the chapel of the Blessed Virgin Mary in All Saints', in the place where the chorister stood during the services.[140] William Austyn, however, was closely associated with the town's ruling body. He served as mayor in 1459-60, 1467-8 and in 1475-6, and was commonly named as executor, witness or feoffee for other members of the governing elite.[141] His own will was supervised by the gentleman John Chaney, who owned much property in Abington Street and in St Edmund's End, and who was himself buried in the Lady chapel in St Giles' Church. Austyn owned property in Derngate and evidently lived in the parish. His association with All Saints' is further proof of the civic character of that church.[142]

Property deeds and the town rental of 1503-4 provide plentiful evidence of gentry presence in this quarter of Northampton.[143] This will be discussed in more detail below. The archaeological evidence for two substantial stone buildings in Derngate, of which at least one consisted of two or more storeys and had a tiled floor and a stone garderobe behind, and the evidence of a high-status property on The Riding, provides welcome substantiation of the documentary evidence.[144] It is interesting to note that the 'genteel' quarter of nineteenth-century Northampton

---

139 Early Will Register, ff. 19v, 24r, 42v, 46r.

140 Early Will Register, f. 86r.

141 Early Will Register, ff. 6r, 8v, 13v, 28r, 50v.

142 Early Will Register, ff. 28r, 90r-91r.

143 NRO, Royal Charter 29.

144 Williams and Farwell, 'The Riding'.

developed on the eastern side of the town, with middle-class housing springing up along Billing Road and Cliftonville. This was partly because the Nene valley was liable to flooding and this restricted growth to the south and to the west of the town. Moreover, the shoe industry was still unmechanised and there was thus no danger of smoke being carried eastwards by the prevailing winds.[145]

St Gregory's Church – This stood in the south-western quarter of Northampton, not far from the church of St Peter. The five surviving wills indicate that this parish too was the home of craftsmen and artisans. Among the testators were a fuller, a tanner, a dyer and a baker. The fifth man, for whom no occupation was given, left rent from a tenement with *tentura fulloniu'* in the parish to the church guild, suggesting that he too was involved in textiles.[146] The will of a second baker buried in St Gregory's was proved in the Prerogative Court of Canterbury.[147] Witnesses named in the wills included weavers, fullers, a dyer, a baker and a master of the *scolarum gram'ti.*

The church contained a chapel of St Katherine; an early-sixteenth-century will mentioned a chapel of Our Lady.[148] The fraternity of the Holy Rood in the Wall was based in St Gregory's. This guild was founded in 1472 by the knights William Lord Hastings and Ralph Hastings, to celebrate divine service for the good estate of the king and queen and their descendants, for the souls of the founders and the guild brethren, and for the souls of the king's father and his progenitors.[149] In Leicester the small but relatively wealthy guild of Holy Trinity with an altar in the church of St Mary de Castro was founded by Sir Richard Sacheverell c.1495. It

---

145 J. Steane, *The Northamptonshire Landscape* (London, 1974), 270. Steane contrasts Bolton, Manchester and Birmingham where the middle-class areas developed to the south-west.

146 Early Will Register, ff. 15r, 30v, 89v, 110r, 152v.

147 PRO, PROB 11/14, 1 Holgrave (f. 4v).

148 Serjeantson and Longden, 'Parish churches of Northamptonshire', 378-9.

149 *Calendar of Patent Rolls* (1467-1477), 372.

numbered the local gentry among its membership; Henry Lord Hastings provided venison for the feast in some years.[150] It seems possible that such guilds were a feature of top-ranking towns, providing congenial company for visiting gentlemen and possibly a means of displaying power and lordship. In Northampton the church of St Mary's by the Castle was not chosen by the guild founders to house the fraternity's altar. This could be interpreted as a reflection of the declining fortunes of the area and the continuing neglect of the castle. It is difficult to understand, however, why St Gregory's Church was chosen to house this fraternity, which was mentioned in the wills of many townsmen.

The church of the Holy Sepulchre – Only three wills made by parishioners of this church survive in the Early Register, those of a clothier and his widow, and of another widow.[151] The will of a butcher dating from 1500 and proved in the Prerogative Court of Canterbury has also been checked.[152] Little can therefore be said about the church in the later medieval period. This is particularly regrettable since the archaeological interpretation of the development of this church is disputed.[153] There are references to the high altar, to the rood loft, to the altars of the Blessed Virgin Mary and of St Martin, and to the steeple and its bells. Early-sixteenth-century wills recorded chapels of St Nicholas, and of St Thomas and St John the Baptist (seemingly sharing an altar). There was mention also of St Modwen.[154]

The fraternity in Holy Sepulchre was dedicated to St Martin; the fraternity of St Sepulchre, mentioned in 1476, is thought to represent the same guild. This

---

[150] J. Wilshere, *The Religious Gilds of Medieval Leicester* (Leicester, 1979), 24-6.

[151] Early Will Register, ff. 51v, 101r, 111v.

[152] PRO, PROB 11/14, 4 Holgrave (f. 25v). Four wills made by parishioners of Holy Sepulchre and proved at Canterbury have not been searched.

[153] *Vide infra,* 13-14.

[154] Serjeantson and Longden, 'Parish churches of Northamptonshire', 381-2.

fraternity was associated with the town's butchers, whose guild assembled on the Tuesday following Martinmas Day when the outgoing masters rendered their accounts.[155] In 1485 the butcher William Atwell, who was himself buried in the churchyard of All Saints', left two torches worth 13s 4d to the [ ] of St Martin in Holy Sepulchre. In the same year the butcher Richard Duffron, buried in All Saints', left 3s 4d to the fabric of Holy Sepulchre.[156] In 1500 the butcher Thomas Knight asked to be buried before the image of St Martin and left 10s to the saint's altar. The sources therefore suggest a particular association of butchers with Holy Sepulchre, possibly stemming from the church's proximity to the fields beyond the walls.

Thomas Knight was one of two testators who left money to repair the highway between the church and the North Gate; he also left 8d to repair the common well there. The clothier Thomas Whyte was one of the few townsmen who remembered the monks of St Andrew's in his will, two of them being identified by name. The butcher William Atwell left 3s 4d to the priory, and his best gown to his brother, a monk within its walls.[157]

St Mary's and St. Michael's – Three testators requested burial in the chapel of St Katherine in St Mary's Church, among them a weaver and the chaplain of the chantry there.[158] The guild of St Katherine had been founded in 1347 to provide a chaplain to assist the parson, and increased membership had subsequently allowed the appointment of a second chaplain. In 1389, however, the guild described itself as *paupercula fraternitas*; this may reflect the suggested decline in the population

---

[155] *NBR*, vol. I, 337.

[156] Early Will Register, ff. 38v, 40r.

[157] Early Will Register, ff. 40r, 51v.

[158] Early Will Register, ff. 40v, 105v, 121r.

of the parish.[159] None of the three testators remembered the guild in their wills, although it evidently continued in being.[160]

A butcher acted as executor for the chantry chaplain in 1500. The bequest to St Mary's Church 'next to the king's castle' made by the butcher Edward Atwell in 1485 raises the possibility that the area contained empty ground which may have been used by butchers to graze their animals prior to slaughter.[161] In 1502 the weaver Thomas Hendyman, who asked to be buried in St Peter's churchyard, willed that his garden (*ortus*) next to the castle known as 'the castel grene' be sold and the money raised distributed to the poor.[162]

In the Feudal Aid of 1428 St Mary's and St Michael's each contributed £2; in 1535 the value of St Mary's was set at £2 13s 4d, but that of St Michael's was only 16s 7d, the lowest value of all the parish churches.[163] This decline was perhaps a result of falling population and helps to explain why the parish was absorbed into the parish of Holy Sepulchre after the Reformation.[164] Two wills in the Early Register were made by parishioners of St Michael's: in 1482 John Asplond asked to be buried in the churchyard and left sixpence to the church fabric; in 1505 John Cobbe requested burial before the image of the Blessed Virgin in the church and left 6s 8d for repairs.[165] In the last quarter of the fifteenth century a number of townspeople who lived in other parts of Northampton also remembered St Michael's in their

---

159 Westlake, *Parish Gilds*, Appendix, no. 382.

160 Serjeantson and Longden, 'Parish churches of Northamptonshire', 379-80; also noted here are the lights of St John the Baptist, of the Trinity, of the Sacrament and of the Sepulchre.

161 Early Will Register, f. 39r. In 1490 Edward Atwell was tenant of a croft in the parish of Holy Sepulchre, in an area of crofts and gardens (*ibid.*, f. 92v).

162 Early Will Register, f. 147r.

163 Williams, *Saxon and Medieval Northampton*, 47.

164 RCHM, *Northampton*, 56.

165 Early Will Register, ff. 29v, 183v-184r.

wills, and made gifts of money (typically 3s 4d) either for repairs or for the fraternity based in the church. A cloth painted with angels was bequeathed to the church by a dyer's widow in 1480.[166] In 1513 a bequest of 20s was made for building the steeple.[167]

The Suburban Churches – Documentary evidence for the churches which served Northampton's suburbs is too scanty for meaningful discussion. St Bartholomew's, to the north of the town, had lost its parochial status at an early date, and the sole late-fifteenth-century reference found so far mentions the chapel as a geographical reference point.[168] One will survives for a parishioner of St Leonard's in Cotton, and one for St Edmund's in St Edmund's End. The latter demonstrates the pre-eminence of All Saints' in the town, for although Thomas Symson left 3s 4d to his parish church he asked that his horn should be given to the chapel of Corpus Christi 'to remain there for ever to the use of Robyn Hood to have every Whitsun Monday and all other times when he need it'.[169] No wills for parishioners of St Margaret's Church in St James' End are recorded in the Early Register, although a few are quoted by Serjeantson and Longden.[170]

Religious Institutions

The provision of religious institutions in Northampton clearly reflected the town's importance in the early middle ages and indicated the town's continuing top ranking in the urban hierarchy of its shire in the later medieval period. St Andrew's Priory, founded for Cluniac monks in c.1100, occupied a large site

---

166 Early Will Register, ff. 7v, 16v, 27v, 48v, 50r, 53r, 111v-112r, 158r.

167 Serjeantson and Longden, 'Parish churches of Northamptonshire', 380-1.

168 Serjeantson and Longden, 'Parish churches of Northamptonshire', 379: 'the highway outside the North Gate leading to the chapel of St Bartholomew'.

169 Early Will Register, ff. 123v, 129r.

170 Serjeantson and Longden, 'Parish churches of Northamptonshire', 379: mention of the light before St Margaret and of the altar of St Katherine.

within the walls in the northern quarter of the town. Outside the West Gate stood St James' Abbey, a house of Austin canons founded at the beginning of the twelfth century. In the meadows to the south of the town was the convent of St Mary de la Pre, a Cluniac nunnery established in c.1145. The houses of St Andrew's and of St James were frequently used for monastic gatherings. At least twenty of the triennial general chapters of the Austin Canons were held in St James' Abbey between 1237 and 1446; thirty-nine of the forty general chapters of the Benedictines between 1338 and 1498 were held at St Andrew's, although it was a Cluniac house. During the parliament of 1380, because of the poor state of the castle, sessions were held in the priory. In the seventeenth century it was alleged that both houses had entertained travellers before the Reformation, because of the poor quality of the town's inns. Travellers coming from the west were lodged in the abbey, while those coming from the north found shelter in the priory.[171]

All four main orders of friars (Dominicans, Franciscans, Carmelites and Augustinians) were attracted to Northampton, and all were granted land for their precincts within the walls. Houses of the friars of the Sack and of the Poor Clares existed in the town for a few years in the thirteenth century. A provincial chapter was held in the house of the Dominicans in 1239, and the royal chancery was established in their church from 31 July - 6 August 1338. Four provincial chapters were held in the Carmelites' Church in the fourteenth century.[172] The Hospital of St John, founded in c.1138, stood on the east side of Bridge Street, near the South Gate. Just beyond this gate was the Hospital of St Thomas, apparently founded in the fifteenth century. The hermitage of St Thomas was located in Cotton End, on the southern side of the bridge. Also in Cotton End was the leper hospital of St

---

[171] *VCH, Northamptonshire*, vol. III, 35, 58. From at least 1498 Coventry usurped the place of Northampton as the periodic venue for provincial chapters of the Black Monks: C. Phythian-Adams, *Desolation of a City: Coventry and the Urban Crisis of the Late Middle Ages* (Cambridge, 1979), 21.

[172] *VCH, Northamptonshire*, vol. III, 57-9; Williams, *Saxon and Medieval Northampton*, 48-9.

Leonard's, founded before 1150; this hospital acquired parochial rights in the thirteenth century. There may also have been a hermitage on the west bridge of the town.[173]

Approximately one quarter of the intra-mural area of Northampton was occupied by the religious houses. At the Dissolution St Andrew's Priory owned over 100 houses and shops within the town, and St James' Abbey owned over 60, a total representing perhaps one third of such property. It has been suggested that, like other monastic establishments elsewhere in Northamptonshire, the abbey actively promoted urban development.[174] St Andrew's also held the advowsons of all the parish churches. Its wealth was perhaps one reason why the priory enjoyed little popularity; few townspeople remembered the monks in their wills, and then only for tithes forgotten.[175] The notary Richard Green was more generous and gave the priory £3. One man requested burial in the monastery, and two others left bequests to individual monks.[176] The nuns also received few bequests, and only one burial in the convent church is recorded in the Register Book.[177] The weavers' ordinances of 1432 indicate that the convent may have played a part in the ceremonial life of their craft. An Easter procession to St Mary de la Pre to offer wax tapers was described as an old-established custom, to be followed by customable drinking.[178]

There is a little more evidence for the abbey of St James, described by Leland as standing 'a little distant from the extreme part of the west suburb. 'The waulle that

---

173 *VCH, Northamptonshire*, vol. III, 59-61; G. Foard, 'The Early Topography of Northampton and its Suburbs', *Northamptonshire Archaeology*, 26 (1995), 117-19.

174 RCHM, *Northampton*, 56; Williams, *Saxon and Medieval Northampton*, 50; Foard, 'Early Topography', 118.

175 E.g., Early Will Register, ff. 37v, 41v, 44v, 46v, 50v, 93v, 95r.

176 PRO, PROB 11/14, 7 Holgrave (f. 49v); Early Will Register, ff. 40r, 51v, 81v .

177 BL, Add. Ch. 735; Early Register Book, ff. 6r, 7v, 22v, 26r, 50r. The latest bequest dates from 1487.

178 *NBR*, vol. I, 268-74.

cumpasith the hole site of the house is highe, faire, and large, *ex lapide quadrato*'.[179] Much of the abbey's property was located in St James' End. The rental of 1332 listed c. 31 tenements in this suburb, for which the rent was paid to *cam'am con* [ ], and perhaps another 17 tenants who paid rent either to the almoner or to the altar of the Holy Rood.[180] The abbey had been granted a yearly fair on St James' day (25 July) in 1268. It was held in St James' End and was said to have led to much friction with the townspeople. At the Dissolution, by which time the expenses were said to cancel out the profits, it became a town fair.[181]

Two people are known to have requested burial in the abbey church: the widow of William Tresham *armiger* in 1479, and the tanner John Buckby in 1485. He was perhaps the bailiff of Northampton in 1482, and as a relatively wealthy man able to afford to pay the abbey 40s for his burial.[182] It would seem that only the wealthiest townspeople left bequests to the abbey; just seven bequests are recorded in the Register Book, all of them made by testators who cast their pious offerings very widely, naming all or most of Northampton's religious institutions.[183]

The less affluent burgesses appear to have considered that the enclosed orders were sufficiently well-endowed. Forty-three testators, however, left small bequests to the four friaries in the town, commonly leaving the same amount to each order. The Friars Minor were singled out by three testators, and the Carmelites similarly benefited from preferential treatment in three wills.[184] In 1481 Thomas Merton, a parishioner of St Gregory's, left 6s 8d to 'the poor brothers of the Augustinian

---

[179] L. Toulmin Smith (ed.), *The Itinerary of John Leland in or About the Years 1535-1543*, Parts I to III (London, 1907), 7.
[180] BL, Add. Ch. 6117.
[181] *VCH, Northamptonshire*, vol. III, 24.
[182] Early Will Register, ff. 23r, 42v.
[183] Early Will Register, ff. 6r, 22v, 46v, 50r, 86r, 90r, 101r.
[184] Early Will Register, ff. 13v, 50v, 99r (Friars Minor); ff. 51v, 52r, 183v-184r (Carmelites).

order' whose house stood close to his church. The innholder Hugo Wodfall in 1490 excused the Austin friars the 60s they owed him for ale, on condition that they celebrated a requiem mass in his memory. Some years later a capper left 4d to each friar of this order.[185] Only one Northampton burgess asked for the town's friars to participate in his funeral: the influential William Perwyn, bailiff of 1494 and father of the mayor of 1509.[186] This may be contrasted with Leicester, where the leading townsmen not uncommonly requested all three orders of friars 'to bring their body to the grave'.[187] Visiting traders also remembered Northampton's friars in their wills. In 1518, for example, a man from Market Harborough left 10s to the 'Black Friars in the horsemarket' to celebrate a trental of masses.[188]

The steady trickle of bequests recorded in the surviving wills helps to explain the fifteenth-century work on the cloisters and the re-tiling of the floor of the Franciscan friary, described by Leland as 'the beste buildid and largest house of all the places of the freres'.[189] The friaries may also have benefited from association with Northampton's craft guilds. The 1427 ordinances for the shearmen laid down that the craft was to gather on All Souls' day (2 November) at the White Friars to choose two wardens for the coming year. The light of the town's heliers (roofers) and slaters burned before the image of Our Lady in the church of the Friars Preachers.[190] Another source of income may have been the use of their precincts for storage. In 1504 the notary Richard Grene had timber in a 'lean-to' at the Grey Friars.[191] The anchorite living in the house of the Augustinians received several

---

[185] Early Will Register, ff. 30v-31r, 92r-92v, 135v-136r.

[186] Early Will Register, f. 81v.

[187] LRO, First Register Book of Wills, ff. 79-79v, 82-3, 193-5, 331v, 419v-420.

[188] LRO, Second Register Book of Wills, ff. 43-43v.

[189] *Vide infra*, 26-7; Leland, *Itinerary*, 9.

[190] *NBR*, vol. I, 329-30, 356. In Coventry the tilers' craft had special arrangements with the White Friars (Phythian-Adams, *Desolation*, 138).

[191] PRO, PROB 11/14, 7 Holgrave (f. 49v). In Chester the poverty of the Franciscans led to them allowing the nave and three aisles of their church to be used from 1528 for the storage

bequests in the early sixteenth century. The occasional elite burial should not be forgotten. In 1515 Sir Everard Fielding knight was buried before the altar in the church of the Dominicans, and in 1529 his widow was buried by his side.[192]

The surviving wills indicate that although most Northampton townspeople thought first of the religious fraternities based in their parish churches, they often remembered the hospitals of St Thomas and of St John. The almshouse of St Thomas had been founded but recently; interest and enthusiasm among the urban populace were perhaps at their height. St John's had been founded in c.1138, but it underwent much expensive rebuilding in the fourteenth and fifteenth centuries, presumably financed, at least in part, by pious bequests.[193] The earliest surviving will in the Register Book, made by the weaver John Pedder in 1462, included a bequest of 3s 4d to the fraternity of St Thomas the martyr. His was the first of many such gifts, usually in the form of money, but also including linen cloth and assorted metal pots, pewter saucers and candelabra of latten.[194]

St John's Hospital received fewer bequests although it stood within the walls and was occasionally named as the place where wills were proved.[195] In 1493 two weavers asked to be buried in its church, one of them specifying a place in front of the Holy Rood, and the second requesting burial before the altar in the chapel of the Virgin Mary. The hospital received the best of three woollen cloths of russet from one weaver, and the rent from his tenement in Woolmonger Street from the

---

of sails and other nautical equipment (J.H.E. Bennett, 'The Grey Friars of Chester', *Journal of the Chester Archaeological Society*, 24 (1921), 26-9, 31-2).

[192] Serjeantson and Longden, 'Parish churches of Northamptonshire', 446-8. Recorded here is a bequest of 20s in 1502 towards making the steeple of the Dominicans, and one of £10 in 1535 towards building their chancel 'if they build it new'.

[193] *VCH, Northamptonshire*, vol. III, 59-61.

[194] Early Will Register, ff. 7r, 7v, 94r.

[195] E.g., Early Will Register, ff. 81v, 82r. It has been claimed that the hospital of St John was intended for the poor of the county, and that of St Thomas for the townspeople (*VCH, Northamptonshire*, vol. III, 21).

second.[196] Richard Sherd, the master of the hospital, acted as supervisor of one of these wills. His picture can be seen in the surviving building, in the window lighting the staircase; his will, made in 1503, is recorded in the Register Book. He had retired by this time, but he was to be buried in the chancel of the hospital church. Among the possessions in his parlour and chamber (which had a chimney) were two Stourbridge coffers, a press, a close chair, a head of St John, and a pair of tables with their men.[197]

Northampton's pre-eminence in its shire was epitomised by its ecclesiastical status. The surviving historical evidence does not reveal that the religious institutions themselves created income for the town, but this is probably because no sources survive which detail (for example) employment opportunities for building workers, or local purchases by the religious houses. The ale obtained by the Austin friars from one of the town's innholders, and for which they failed to pay, is the sole example yet traced of commercial inter-action between the religious and lay communities. Yet it would appear certain that Northampton benefited from the presence of the enclosed orders and of the friaries. The finger of St Andrew in the priory doubtless drew pilgrims to the town; St James' fair, although seemingly held beyond the liberties, attracted customers who would have ventured within the walls. The abbey built a fulling mill that created work. The friaries received bequests from people who lived in the rural hinterland and who perhaps came to hear them preach or to ask them to pray for them before setting out on a journey.

---

[196] Early Will Register, ff. 98r, 99v.

[197] *VCH, Northamptonshire*, vol. III, 59-60; Early Will Register, f. 154v. *VCH* gives 1474 as the date when Sherd was master, and suggests that this may give an approximate date for the fifteenth-century alterations to the hospital. The evidence of the 1493 wills, however, and of Sherd's own will, indicates that such a suggestion is ill-founded.

Domestic housing and associated commercial elements

Leland visited Northampton between 1535 and 1543, some two decades after the great fire of 1516, which allegedly destroyed most of the town. He noted that the old buildings were of stone and the new ones of timber.[198] In many medieval towns new building in stone was unusual in the later medieval period, and such stone structures as existed were often notable landmarks, relics of an earlier age. The archaeological evidence for Northampton appears to conform to this pattern of development, with thirteenth-century structures built of stone up to first-floor level, and with the houses of the fourteenth and fifteenth centuries consisting of timber-frame construction, resting on dwarf stone walls.[199] Possibly some of the stone came from the quarry near the East Gate, mentioned in the rental dating from the reign of Edward I.

The historical evidence contains little which sheds light on the physical appearance of the houses in the late medieval town. None of the property deeds found to date referred to stone buildings, or gave dimensions of street frontages or length of burgage plots. The early rental recorded various elements of domestic buildings, together with the associated commercial units. Tenements and houses were listed most often, but occasionally rents were given for ovens (*furnum*), chambers (*camera*), halls (*aula*), shops (*schoppa*), stairs (*gradus*), doors or gates (*porta*), and cellars (*cellarium* or *sellarium*). There was mention of a tavern (*taverna*) in Gold Street, and of a solar with cellar in the Drapery, evidently in separate occupation from the tenement which they adjoined, thus forming a commercial unit typically found in a prime trading area.[200] The mention of stairs is of interest as it may imply external access to an upper storey, as at Tackley's Inn in Oxford, or even to the

---

[198] Leland, *Itinerary*, 7.

[199] *Vide infra*, 16-24, 27-8.

[200] PRO, SC 12/13/38.

existence of an upper walkway, as in the Rows at Chester.[201] One mercer paid 6d for a stairway between his shops. One stairway in Abington Street was described as 'opposite' a seld. The 1332 rental of St James' Abbey included two rents (each of 3s) from tenants under the seld (*sub selda*), probably in Abington Street.[202] This seld may perhaps have been a bazaar-like structure, as found in London's Cheapside.[203]

Marginal entries listed the streets in which the property lay. They indicated that cellars were found in St Giles' Street, in the Drapery, and near to the Franciscan friary. The 1503-4 rental recorded only the cellar and solar in the Drapery.[204] One medieval vaulted undercroft still remains, on George Row, just south of All Saints'. Similar arched cellars in the Drapery and at the south-western end of College Street survived into the nineteenth century.[205] The rental of Edward I listed a rent of 16d *pro Bello fronte* in St Giles' Street, a rent of 16d for *Bello fronte Cokkes*[ ] in the Row where [ ] and 'dredge' were sold, and 8d for the *Bello fronte* opposite a garden in the North Quarter. All three were included in the 1503-4 rental, although the *bello fronte voc' cokysauche* in the Row where oats, barley and dredge were sold had by this time been divided into two.[206] The western part was occupied by a shoemaker, and a second shoemaker occupied the other corner, each of them paying 8d in rent. It seems likely that such structures were found only in large towns.

---

[201] A.N. Brown (ed.), *The Rows of Chester* (English Heritage, 1999).

[202] BL, Add. Ch. 6117.

[203] D. Keene, 'Shops and Shopping in Medieval London', in *Medieval Art, Architecture and Archaeology in London* (British Archaeological Association, 1990), 38-40.

[204] NRO, Royal Charter 29, m. 1d.

[205] *Vide infra,* 15-16.

[206] Mike Shaw suggests that *Bello Fronte* may have been a house name.

The 1332 rental of St James' Abbey listed a rent of 8d for a solar 'in which bread was sold' in the parish of All Saints', and a rent of 1d for a solar *ad corbell.*[207] In 1358 a capital messuage with shops opposite All Saints' was described as extending from the adjoining tenement by a long chamber over the shops (*per longam cameram super shopas*); a shop with an upper chamber was leased to a man and wife in 1382; a shop with chambers and houses 'above bielded' set in the old Drapery was leased to a mercer in 1455; and in 1499 two tenements with three 'ruffis' and their appurtenances 'set together' at the corner of the Chequer were leased to a saddler and his wife.[208] An extent dating from 1419-20 mentioned a shop with chamber above in the Mercers' Row.[209] This evidence suggests intensive use of space and indicates something of the commercial pressures operating in prime trading areas.

Some testators mentioned rooms in their wills and thus provided a little information about the domestic accommodation of private houses. In 1487 the widow Alice Peny bequeathed beds and other items in the hall chamber, the middle chamber and in a third chamber, and also referred to goods in the 'melyng' house and in the brew-house. Her house perhaps stood in Swinewell Street. The home of Isbell Geffray, with its cheese chamber, may have been in the same area.[210] In 1500 George Dyk mentioned furniture in the chamber, little parlour and hall.[211] The hall was the room most commonly named, and there was occasional reference to its hearth.[212] The medieval house-plan with a hall, often open to the roof, and with chambers at one end and a kitchen block at the other, continued in use in

[207] BL, Add. Ch. 6117.

[208] *Catalogue of Ancient Deeds*, vol. II, B 2463; vol. IV, A 7651; A 8107; vol. V, A 10945.

[209] PRO, E 142/84.

[210] Early Will Register, ff. 52r, 75v; NRO, Royal Charter 29, m. 1: property here held by her son in 1503-4.

[211] Early Will Register, f. 82r.

[212] Early Will Register, ff. 27r-27v, 86r, 102r, 106v, 116r.

gentry houses in Northamptonshire into the sixteenth century.[213] It would seem that the hall served as the main living accommodation for the townspeople of Northampton in the second half of the fifteenth century and first decades of the sixteenth century. The hall may also have been used for craft activities. The shoemaker John Apryse and the fuller William Halowton each had counters standing in their hall. Halowton's home contained a shop where his walkers' earth and burling irons were kept. The dyer Simon Brafeld kept his dyestuffs in his house; and the fuller Nicholas Bowker, who lived outside the South Gate, had a workhouse within his house.[214]

Relatively few building workers are attested in the documentary sources, indicative perhaps of their lowly status within the community. William Carpenter of St James' was named in the estreat roll dating from the reign of Edward I; John Daubour, Simon Pavour and John Carpenter were tenants of the abbey in 1332.[215] Masons were named in an eyre roll of 1329; the fragment of the 1381 poll-tax list recorded two carpenters, a dauber and a plumber's servant.[216] Only the carpenter William Jonson made a will that survives. In 1504 he requested burial in St Giles' Church, left his house in Knight Street to his wife for her lifetime, named Master and Mistress Lole as overseers and asked them to be good master and mistress to his wife. This may imply a particular 'working' relationship with the gentleman John Lole, who held tenements in Swinewell Street and St Giles' Street.[217]

The 1503-4 rental listed a thacker outside the West Gate, a stainer with tenements in Newlands and in Bearward Street, two masons renting open ground outside the East Gate (near the quarry), and Christopher Ridyng helier (roofer), tenant of the

---

213 Steane, *Northamptonshire Landscape*, 200.

214 Early Will Register, ff. 97v, 106v, 116r, 117r.

215 'Profits of the court of Northampton', 204; BL, Add. Ch. 6117.

216 *VCH, Northamptonshire*, vol. III, 27; PRO, E 179/155/41.

217 Early Will Register, ff. 165r-165v; NRO, Royal Charter 29.

inn called the Bell in Swinewell Street and bailiff of Northampton in 1499-1500.[218] The estreat roll for Chequer Ward in 1520-1 recorded fines imposed on a carpenter, a mason, a painter, a paver and the helier Robert Thacker; in the same year three heliers and two pavers living in the parish of St Giles and in St Edmund's End were also amerced.[219] More building workers contributed to the subsidy of 1524, including several men assessed on wages of 20s: 6 heliers and 3 servants, 5 plumbers, 5 masons, 4 carpenters, 3 painters and their 2 servants. Two plumbers each assessed at £20 were the wealthiest building craftsmen; no other building craftsman had goods exceeding £4.[220] The number of heliers attested in the subsidy suggests that demand for their skills had possibly increased in the years following the fire of 1516; alternatively it may be that tax was then demanded from less affluent townsmen.

Two joiners paid tax in 1524, and perhaps made items of furniture like those recorded in the wills. Northampton's homes were furnished with tables, chests, coffers, cupboards and chairs. Tables were described as folding (*plicabile* or *duplicata*) or were provided with trestles. Chests came in varying sizes, and were usually made of spruce. Alice Peny's home contained two painted chests. Beds stood in the chambers, with coverings of tapestry or with coverings embroidered with white lilies, or with red and green lions.[221] The wealthiest homes had painted hangings on the walls of the hall and parlour. (Three painters and two painters' servants paid tax in 1524). Margaret Hancock, widow of a dyer and former mayor, had hangings painted with angels and garlands near the hearth in her hall. These were to be divided into three parts and given to the hospitals of St John and of St

---

[218] NRO, Royal Charter 29. A distinguishing feature of innkeepers in Exeter was their widespread involvement in occupations outside innkeeping - including roofing - suggesting that they depended upon servants and family labour to run their inns: M. Kowaleski, *Local Markets and Regional Trade in Medieval Exeter* (Cambridge, 1995), 144.

[219] NRO, Royal Charters 30, 31 (one paver was named in both wards).

[220] PRO, E 179/155/124; Dyer, 'Northampton in 1524', 73-80.

[221] E.g., Early Will Register, ff. 15r-16r, 22v, 52r, 82r, 94r, 102r, 111r, 121r, 123v-124r.

Thomas and to the church of St Michael. Another hanging, painted with pictures of St John the Baptist, St Christopher and St John the Evangelist, was bequeathed to a relative.[222]

Small finds recorded in the reports of excavations in Northampton include much pottery and scraps of metal indicating the manufacture of pins and lace tags.[223] Such items do not feature in the documentary sources. Testators were concerned not with items of little intrinsic value, but with silver plate, with household wares made of metal, and with costly gowns and girdles. In 1475 the bequests of William Haryson, parishioner of St Gregory's Church, included eleven silver spoons, a rosary with silver beads, a large number of bowls, dishes and pots of brass, several latten candlesticks, two pewter salts with covers, and some pewter dishes and saucers. There were pewter vessels that could hold a pottle of ale, and a pint vessel for wine. Among the kitchenware were a large cauldron, several iron spits and 'gobberds', a skillet, a skimmer, a chafing dish and a flesh-hook. A skillet was used for boiling meat, whereas a spit was used for roasting it. The presence of spits in Haryson's home suggests that his was a relatively wealthy household in which the more expensive joints of meat were consumed.

Occupational areas of Northampton

Excavations on street frontage sites have allowed the basic pattern of occupation in the medieval town to be determined, and have also furnished evidence for changing patterns of domestic wealth. Archaeology suggests that St Peter's Street was not particularly wealthy in the fifteenth century, whereas a house in Derngate was

---

[222] Early Will Register, ff. 27r-27v, 154r.
[223] *Vide infra*, 37.

floored with expensive ceramic tiles.[224] The documentary evidence corroborates these findings.

As indicated in the section on Northampton's parish churches, the parish of St Giles was marked by a strong gentry presence. All the gentlemen and squires attested in the wills were associated with this parish either by chosen place of burial and/or by particular bequests to its church. Their families were linked by marriage.[225] Other gentlemen either lived or held property in the same part of town. In 1480, for example, a wealthy widow asked that her garden be given to the gentleman William Austyn and his wife. This garden lay next to the Derngate with a garden belonging to the squire William Catesby on the west and a garden formerly belonging to Thomas Tresham knight on the north.[226] The gentleman John Chaney, whose wife received a bequest from Margaret Harowden and who himself supervised the will of William Austyn, owned two tenements with adjacent garden in Abington Street, a barn and garden in the same street, and a tower called Latymer Tower with its four adjoining gardens, two closes and yard. This tower stood in Swinewell Street.[227]

More evidence for gentry property in the parish can be found in the 1503-4 rental. In Swinewell Street the manor of Gobion was held by John Turpyn gentleman. Other property in the street was held by the gentlemen John Harrold, John Tresham, John Lole, Robert Power, [ ] Lub'nam, and by Richard Benson knight. The squire William Catesby held two houses, a hall and a gate in St Giles' Street.

---

[224] *Vide infra*, 16-17, 29.

[225] E.g., Margaret Harowden, who was living in St Giles' parish at the time of her death, was the sister of Isabella Peche (widow of William Tresham *armiger*) and of Thomas Mauteby *armiger*; she herself had been married to Richard Harowden *armiger*, and her daughter was married to George Longvyle (Early Will Register, ff. 19v, 23r, 24r, 46r).

[226] Early Will Register, f. 28r.

[227] Early Will Register, ff. 90r-91r. Chaney held much other property as well (NRO, Royal Charter 29).

It would seem that the houses were not always occupied by these gentlemen on a regular basis but were instead leased to townsfolk. Some may have served as inns.[228] Private charters and leases also indicate gentry property holdings in the parish.[229] In 1503-4 the gentry held property in other parts of Northampton, including an inn in Bridge Street known as the Angel, and a tenement with shops in Gold Street called the Cardinal's Hat. They also owned shops in the Drapery and shambles in the Butchers' Row. William Catesby held two shambles on the northern side of the Row. This suggests that he perhaps used Northampton as an outlet for some of the stock raised on the family's Warwickshire estates, an interesting indication of the character of the contacts between rural gentlemen and the town. It seems clear, however, that although the gentry had commercial interests in the town centre, they chose the eastern quarter for their residences. Testators with large houses and expensive furnishings, like Margaret Hancock, Alice Peny, Isbell Geffray and John Chaney, all lived in the parish of St Giles. The documents therefore dovetail neatly with the archaeology. This is the area of Northampton where houses with expensive ceramic floors and stone garderobes may be expected.

The wills of testators from the parishes of St Peter's and St Gregory's tell a different story. In 1467 a mercer left property in Woolmonger Street to his wife; it had once been held by a squire and consisted of five cottages *sive* stables with chambers and adjacent gardens.[230] A lease of 1361 mentioned five shops set together beneath a tenement in Goldsmith Street, belonging to the knight John Paynel Gobyon and which he now leased to Adam le Cardemaker and his wife.[231] Archaeology has shown that there was metal-working in nearby Marefair, and in St

---

[228] See below for section on inns.

[229] E.g., NRO, Private Charters 17, 40, 42; *Catalogue of Ancient Deeds*, vol. II, B 2465.

[230] Early Will Register, f. 1v.

[231] NRO, Private Charter 39.

Peter's Street.[232] The wills of other testators from the two parishes contained little information about their homes. None of them mentioned individual rooms, which suggests that the houses were perhaps simple in plan. Not that the testators were poor. The fuller Hugo Hopwood, who asked to be buried in St Peter's Church in 1479, left a silver-gilt bowl worth £6 to his children; a tanner buried in St Gregory's in 1490 bequeathed a piece of silver with a 'pounced' cover to his executor.[233] The majority of these testators were craftsmen, who perhaps considered silver plate a good investment but whose ambitions did not run to painted hangings.

The documentary evidence for these two parishes again corroborates the archaeological findings. Of the nine testators from St Peter's parish, three were tanners, one was the sister of a tanner and one the widow of a shoemaker; several other tanners acted as witnesses. Small wonder that part of the parish was known as 'le Barkers end'. A tenement there was mentioned in a will of 1476, but the name was already current in 1460, when two cottages there lately bought from John Harcourt of West Haddon (some ten miles to the north-west of Northampton) were bequeathed to the fraternities of Holy Trinity and of Corpus Christi in All Saints' Church.[234] In 1485 a tanner supervised the will of the tanner John Bukby of St James' End; among his bequests were ten dickers of 'over ledyr' and 'sole ledyr', and ten cartloads of bark.[235] A lease of 1382 indicates that bark may have commonly been stored in the area. In that year a tenement outside the West Gate

---

[232] *Vide infra*, 37.

[233] Early Will Register, ff. 23r, 89v.

[234] Early Will Register, ff. 16v, 18r, 48r, 123v, 158v; NRO, Private Charter 50. The sources consistently styled the men 'barkers'. At Leicester there were references to tanners and to barkers in the 1330s and 1340s, but by the later 14th century it seems that all the tanners were called barkers: J. Cherry, 'Leather', in J. Blair and N. Ramsey (eds.), *English Medieval Industries* (London, 1991), 307.

[235] Early Will Register, ff. 42v-43r. The names of two influential families of barkers - Harpole and Buckby - were derived from settlements to the west of Northampton.

next to the ditch of running water was leased to a couple from 'Hampslap', with the landlord reserving for himself the chamber on the west of the hall, 'le Barkhouse', and partial easement of the hall, bakehouse and curtilage there.[236] In his will made in 1487 the barker Richard Horpoll left his house with its mill and orchard to his wife, but specified that his brother William, also a barker, should have free access to the pond. In 1500 William's access to the pond yard was confirmed.[237] Three major tanning complexes of c.1550 date have been identified at St Peter's Street and the Green; the documents suggest, however, that tanning had by then long been practised in the area, although alongside domestic occupation.[238]

The fuller Hugo Hopwood and the weaver Thomas Hendyman were also parishioners of St Peter's Church. Hopwood's wife was sister of Richard and William Horpoll; the latter supervised the will of Hendyman.[239] Hopwood and Hendyman were, however, engaged in textile crafts, which the historical evidence indicates were also concentrated in the south-western quarter of Northampton, with the parish of St Gregory's perhaps their main focus. The five testators who sought burial in St Gregory's Church included a fuller and a dyer. A third man held a tenement in the parish with an adjoining *tentura fulloniu'*, which had formerly been in the tenure of a Londoner but which was then in the tenure of a local fuller. The fourth testator was the tanner John Buckby senior, whose will was witnessed by two weavers and a fuller. The final testator was a baker, for whom two fullers

---

[236] NRO, Private Charter 43.

[237] Early Will Register, ff. 48r, 123v. Was the mill a bark-grinding mill? This could indicate a large-scale establishment. The 1503-4 rental listed a fish-pond (*vivarium*) in St Peter's parish held by Richard Horpoll (NRO, Royal Charter 29, m. 1v).

[238] *Vide infra,* 21-3, 38-9. For a full discussion of the documentary sources for the tanning complex, see Shaw, 'The Green, Northampton', 108-12.

[239] Early Will Register, ff. 23r, 147r.

acted as witnesses.[240] Presumably the fullers worked at the fulling mill built by St James' Abbey.[241]

There is evidence that the town's dyers gravitated to the south quarter of Northampton, doubtless because of the ready availability of water from the river. The area of the southern suburb of the town consisted of a group of small islands on the alluvial floodplain between the multiple channels of the Nene. The main river channel formed the boundary on the south and on the west; on the northern side was a subsidiary channel and the town ditch, separating the suburb from the town wall.[242] In 1439 waste ground at the South Gate near the bridge was granted by the mayor, bailiffs, and whole community to sixteen townsmen. It lay between the walls and the ditch of running water, and power to build houses on the ground and over the ditch was also granted.[243]

Four dyers made wills that survive; three of these men had held the mayoralty and numbered among the town's leading men.[244] Two former mayors were buried in the chapel of Corpus Christi, and the third was buried in the chapel of the Blessed Virgin Mary. They followed a long tradition of dyers playing a leading role in civic government. The dyer Pentecost de Kershalton was mayor at least five times at the end of the thirteenth century and in the first decade of the fourteenth century. John le Waydour was mayor in 1322; eight dyers served as bailiff in the years 1386-1461.[245]

---

240 Early Will Register, ff. 15r, 30v, 89v, 110r, 152v.

241 The abbey's fulling mills were at Billing and Cotton Marsh (Steane, *Northamptonshire Landscape*, 113).

242 Foard, 'Early Topography', 118.

243 NRO, Private Charter 48. One piece of ground, measuring 18 yards (by the tailors' yard) by 5 yards lay on the west side of the bridge; a second and third piece, each 28 yards by 4 yards, lay on the east side. Note that John Glover held the adjoining land.

244 John Hancock 1478 (Early Will Register, f. 20r), William Mylle 1492 (*ibid.*, ff. 95r-95v), Simon Brayfeld 1492 (*ibid.*, f. 97v), William Waren 1496 (*ibid.*, f. 106v).

245 *VCH, Northamptonshire*, vol. III, 26.

Northampton had been noted for the dyeing of cloth since the thirteenth century at least. In 1202 it was one of eleven towns that purchased the right to buy and sell cloth as they had done in the reign of Henry, i.e. without keeping the assize of 1197. Regulations concerning the dyeing and weaving of cloth were recorded in the thirteenth-century custumal; they indicated advanced development in technique and in organisation, with both weavers and dyers working with other men's material. Woaders from outside the town were to bring in woad and sell it only by licence of inspectors; all dyers were forbidden from throwing their waste products into the streets. Local tradition, according to Morton writing in 1712, asserted that London cloth had formerly been sent to Northampton to be dyed, and that cloth miscoloured at Nottingham was brought to a good scarlet in the town. Scarlet Well was first mentioned in 1239, and the Eyre Roll of 1247 recorded the death of a dyer, scalded by falling into a vat of his own dye.[246] The fact that woad had been extensively grown in the county in the Anglo-Saxon period possibly helps to explain the prominence of the industry in the medieval town.[247] The availability of a good supply of the running water essential to the craft helped determine the south side of Northampton as the focus of dyeing activity.

The dyer William Mylle held a close and garden in Bridge Street; nearby was a backyard held by another dyer, and a third dyer held a tenement with a garden in the same street.[248] In his will Mylle mentioned the house in which he lived outside the South Gate; this house, together with the leads, vats and other vessels, was left to his wife. The section of the 1503-4 rental listing property outside the South Gate

---

246 *VCH, Northamptonshire*, vol. III, 26.

247 Steane, *Northamptonshire Landscape*, 73. In the eighteenth century Morton considered that Northamptonshire, of all the Midland counties, was the one that 'either is, or has been, woaded most'. Steane takes the place-names Wadcroft, Wadground, Wad Cabin, Wadborough and Wadhill as indicative of the cultivation of woad in the Anglo-Saxon period.

248 Early Will Register, f. 90v. The property was actually owned by the gentleman John Chaney.

noted a tenement once held by the dyer Henry Colman, a house formerly occupied by two dyers in succession, and two tenements near the town ditch held by the heirs of Simon Brayfeld. In 1492 Brayfeld bequeathed all the woad, madder and alum in his house to his wife.[249] Dyers needed a place to dump the waste from the dye-vat, and it is possible that future excavations at Northampton could identify wharfside dumps of madder and weld similar to those identified in Bristol.[250] From the 1460s Northampton was listed in the Brokage Books of Southampton as a major destination for dyestuffs. Amounts of woad were not large compared to amounts destined for (e.g.) London and Coventry: 48 balets in 1460-1, as compared with London (2485) and Coventry (695); 65 balets in 1467-8, as compared with London (908) and Coventry (233).[251] Nevertheless, the amounts indicated a relatively vigorous industry, while the status of the dyers in the second half of the fifteenth century also suggested a successful undertaking. Perhaps the craft declined in subsequent years. Nine dyers were recorded in the 1524 subsidy, but only four in 1525. In 1524 only one dyer was assessed on goods (valued at £5); two were assessed on wages of 33s 4d, five on wages of 20s, and the ninth on lands valued at 20s. The number of dyers assessed on wages in 1524 could help to explain the fall to just four dyers in the following year, three of them assessed on wages.[252] The industry had evidently declined, and although one or two men could earn above-average wages, it no longer held much attraction for the leading burgesses.

Archaeological evidence for metal-working has been found in the western quarter of Northampton.[253] Metal-workers are attested in the documents from an early

---

[249] NRO, Royal Charter 29.

[250] P. Walton, 'Textiles', in *English Medieval Industries*, 337.

[251] O. Coleman (ed.), *The Brokage Book of Southampton 1443-1444*, vol. II (Southampton Records Series, 6, 1961), xxxiv, 323, 324.

[252] PRO, E 179/155/124; Dyer, 'Northampton in 1524', 78.

[253] *Vide infra*, 37.

date. In 1224, when besieging Bedford, Henry III ordered the town's smiths to produce 4,000 quarrels, well-headed and feathered, and 150 good pickaxes. Two cartloads of Gloucester iron were to be sent from Northampton to Bedford for the king's works. A goldsmith was recorded in 1233 and Gold Street in 1330; a knife-smith, a plumber and a lattener were named in the estreat roll of c.1290.[254] In 1322 tenants of St James' Abbey included a smith in St James' End.[255] Four smiths and a plumber's servant were named in the fragment of the 1381 poll tax.[256] Late-fifteenth-century testators included the widow of Richard Ball brazier (1473) and John Butcher wiredrawer (1474); the will of the smith John Hasilbyche dates from 1500.[257] Richard Ball was presumably related to the brazier Simon Ball, bailiff in 1459-60, and his widow had formerly been married to an eminent mercer; Ball himself must have been an influential burgess. He was, however, involved in the mercantile side of the metal trade, as were the three ironmongers who held the mayoralty in the years 1387-1459.[258]

John Butcher wiredrawer asked to be buried in the churchyard of St Giles; John Hasilbyche was buried in the churchyard of All Saints but left the reversion of his term in his house 'on the corner again Holy Sepulchre churchyard' to his wife. In 1425 a property dispute centred on a tenement and annexed cottage called 'le forge'; it lay in Holy Sepulchre Street at the corner of the lane leading towards 'le cappeslane'.[259] A cardmaker was tenant of a house in Whitefriar Lane in 1504.[260] Among those amerced for discarding *scopis* (?house-sweepings) at St Sepulchre's

---

[254] *VCH, Northamptonshire*, vol. III, 27.
[255] BL, Add. Ch. 6117.
[256] PRO, E 179/155/41.
[257] Early Will Register, ff. 7v, 13r, 135r.
[258] John Gregory (1413-14), Thomas Bottesham (1442-3), and Thomas Deraunt (1444-5). The 1503-4 rental listed two shops in the Drapery formerly held by Simon Ball (NRO, Royal Charter 29, m.1d).
[259] BL, Add. Ch. 6057; Eg. Roll 2111.
[260] Early Will Register, f. 188v.

'muckhill' in 1520-1 were a cardmaker, a wiredrawer and a pinner. In the same year the estreat roll for St Edmund's End and for St Giles' parish listed a plumber for a faulty gutter and a smith and his wife for encouraging prostitution.[261] The 1524 subsidy named one ironmonger, two goldsmiths and three pewterers. Eight smiths, five plumbers, three cardmakers, three wiredrawers, a pinner, and a furbisher and his servant also paid tax. The distributive merchants were the wealthiest men involved in the trade. A smith assessed on goods valued at £16, and a smith and a furbisher each assessed on goods worth £5 were the most prosperous of the metal-working craftsmen. Nine men were assessed on wages.[262]

The presence of smiths in a town located on important routeways is understandable. The shoeing of horses was one of the first services sought by many travellers.[263] For this reason smiths' forges were sometimes located near city gates, where they could attract business.[264] The evidence quoted above suggests that some smiths in Northampton may have been based in the suburbs of St Edmund's End and St James' End. It also made sense to place forges outside the walls and therefore minimise the risks from fire.

The historical evidence indicates that some metal-working was carried out in late medieval Northampton, with small items like pins or the cards needed by textile workers the typical products. Metal pots, bowls and candelabra were among the possessions most frequently specified by testators; bronze cauldrons, iron spits, and other kitchen equipment also featured among the bequests.[265] Some of these items

---

[261] NRO, Royal Charters 30, 31.

[262] PRO, E 179/155/124; Dyer, 'Northampton in 1524', 78.

[263] E.g., G.H. Martin, 'Road travel in the Middle Ages: Some Journeys by the Warden and Fellows of Merton College, Oxford, 1315-1470', *Journal of Transport History*, new series, 3 (1975-6), 173-6.

[264] D. Keene, *Survey of Medieval Winchester*, 2 volumes (Oxford, 1985), vol. I, 279-80.

[265] In 1475 the will of the fuller William Haryson listed a great assortment of bronze bowls of different sizes, ewers with lids of tin (*stagnum*), pewter dishes and saucers, latten

may have been purchased at Northampton. In 1501 the draper John Page left his wife all the ironware and treenware in his shop.[266] The sources attest the presence of metal-workers in the eastern quarter of Northampton; so far scant evidence has been found for these craftsmen in the western part of the town. This contrasts with the archaeological evidence for metal-working, most of which came from the western quarter. Some metal-workers were doubtless too poor to appear in the documents. There was no mention of a craft guild for metal-workers in the fifteenth century.

Excavations have revealed a number of grain-drying ovens in St Peter's Street, south of the Green, and at Marefair, as well as two ovens of uncertain function in Swan Street.[267] References to tenements *cum furno* are found in the rentals of the reign of Edward I and of 1503-4.[268] The earlier rental listed an oven at the corner of Cow Lane (the present Swan Street), a tenement with oven in Swinewell Street, another in Abington Street, and an oven in Newlands. The tenement in Abington Street was held by John Eustach, named as a supplier of ale to the royal household during its stay in the town in 1300-1. Eustach was a major supplier, having provided ale worth 20s, and the oven at his tenement may have been associated with making malt.[269] In 1331 two messuages in Abington Street, one with an oven, were leased to a baker and his wife. They were to pay 6s rent each year and 'bake constantly at the said oven'; default of suit to the said oven would make the lease void.[270]

---

candelabra, and an array of cooking equipment; in 1479 a widow's prized possessions included the best chafing-dish with two handles and the bowl called the 'Sonday pott' (Early Will Register, ff. 15r-16r, 22v).

266 Early Will Register, f. 128r.

267 *Vide infra*, 37-8.

268 PRO, SC 12/13/38; NRO, Royal Charter 29.

269 BL, Add. Ch. 75994.

270 *Catalogue of Ancient Deeds*, vol. IV, A 7146; vol. V, A 10870.

All four ovens listed in the early rental were again listed in 1503-4. The one at the corner of Cow Lane was now held by the draper John Adam, occupier of the inn in the Drapery called the Swan. It may have been used for baking horse-bread, an activity commonly undertaken by innkeepers; alternatively, it may have been used for making malt. The tenement with oven in Swinewell Street was associated with 'le Blakhall' in 1503-4; that formerly held by Eustach was in 1503-4 described as lying at the corner of the lane. The later rental listed additional ovens: a *bello fronte* with oven in St Giles' Street owned by the gentleman John Lole; the oven of the mills (*molendinorum*) at the corner of the narrow lane leading from Bridge Street to Kingswell; an oven on the west corner of Gobion's Lane in Abington Street belonging to St James' Abbey; and a tenement with oven under (*subtus*) Kingswell also held by the abbey. This was presumably the oven in Kingswell Street listed in the abbey rental of 1332.[271] It is possible that these ovens may have been commercial enterprises.

Inns

In the thirteenth century Northampton's political and strategic importance, and its great fair, ensured regular influxes of visitors. Attempts were evidently made to accommodate them and to control them during their sojourn. The charter of 1257 provided that during the fairs no foreign merchants were to lodge with their merchandise in the town without the licence of the bailiffs; a deed of 1280 granted a house in Abington Street to a burgess on condition that he provided a kitchen and stabling for nine horses for London burellers during fair-time.[272] In March 1328 the marshals of the royal household were ordered to make proclamation that no

---

[271] BL, Add. Ch. 6117.

[272] *VCH, Northamptonshire*, vol. III, 24. Burellers made a cheap woollen cloth known as burel.

person, at the ensuing parliament at Northampton, was to take lodging without their assent.[273]

Some visitors perhaps stayed in inns, although certain documentary evidence for commercial inns at Northampton is not found before the end of the fifteenth century. At Winchester commercial inns were defined as such in the property records only from the early fifteenth century, although presentations of innkeepers were recorded from 1361.[274] At Northampton references to hostelers and to innkeepers pre-date references to named commercial establishments. Between the years 1452-65, for example, a hosteler was imprisoned for rent arrears and for not repairing a 'place' in the town owned by Richard Verney knight.[275] An ordinance of October 1463 may indicate commercial transactions in inns. Foreign merchants and chapmen (drapers, mercers, hosiers, ironmongers, and flaxmen) who brought any merchandise into town to be sold (excluding victuals) were to show their wares to local merchants and chapmen only within their inns. Hostelers at Exeter often served as middlemen between local and regional traders, partly because inns provided a convenient meeting place.[276]

The wills of four Northampton innholders survive; two other innholders witnessed wills in the 1490s.[277] None of the wills indicated either the size or the fittings of the establishment. John Rychere left a silver spoon to each servant within his house, male and female, 'for their good service'. Hugo Wodfall owned a garden in

---

[273] *Calendar of Patent Rolls* (1327-30), 248.

[274] Keene, *Medieval Winchester*, vol. I, 167.

[275] *Early Chancery Proceedings*, vol. I, bundle 27, no. 213.

[276] *NBR*, vol. I, 300-1. The original document should be checked to ascertain the word translated as 'inn'. A supposed reference to 'inns' in 1397 results from a mis-translation of *ostium* (*ibid.*, 264). Kowaleski, *Local Markets and Regional Trade*, 146.

[277] Early Will Register, ff. 38r (John Rychere 1485), 41v (William Multon 1485), 86v (John Roberdes 1489), 92r-92v (Hugo Wodfall 1490), 100v (John Adam a witness in 1493), 106v (Richard Denton a witness in 1495).

the parish of Holy Sepulchre; this he had leased to the innholder John Adams and to a local shoemaker. Possibly it provided grazing facilities for horses. This would have been valuable to John Adams, recorded in 1503-4 as living in the inn called the Swan in the Drapery, an area where open land may have been in short supply. In 1503-4 Adams also held an oven at the corner of Cow Lane.

Two innholders were named in the 1524 subsidy, one assessed on goods valued at £20, the other on goods worth 10 marks. Some innholders may have been involved in occupations other than innkeeping, as at Exeter, and presumably depended upon servants and family labour.[278] John Adams was also known as John Umfrey draper, and it was as a draper that he was listed in the 1503-4 rental.[279] Five hostelers were named among the taxpayers; four were assessed on wages and one on goods valued at 40s.[280]

Northampton's innholders appear to have sold wine and ale. In 1378-9 one townsman was amerced for having sold ale too dear *infra hospicium*.[281] Hugo Wodfall excused the Augustinian friars the debt of 60s owed to him for ale, on condition that they celebrated a requiem mass for his soul. A vintner witnessed the will of William Multon. In 1529-32 the innholder Ambrose Walker was involved in a dispute over wine with a London ironmonger.[282]

The dispute of 1425-8 involving a tenement called 'le Lyonn' in Holy Sepulchre Lane at the corner of the lane leading towards 'le Cappeslane' provides the earliest

---

278 Kowaleski, *Local Markets and Regional Trade*, 144.

279 Early Will Register, f. 111r: John Adams alias John Umfray draper named as overseer of will of Agnes Roberdes, widow of the innholder John Roberdes.

280 PRO, E 179/155/124. Did they run establishments which were 'down-market' as compared to inns; or did the term 'ostler' indicate a man who attended horses at an inn, a sense to which the term has been restricted since the sixteenth century?

281 NRO, Royal Charter 28, m. 1d.

282 *Early Chancery Proceedings*, vol. VI, bundle 636, no. 55.

reference yet found to a named establishment in Northampton. A cottage known as 'le forge' was annexed to the property and there was also a garden.[283] A rental of the holdings of Catesby Priory in 1428-9 listed a messuage in St Giles' Street in Northampton known as 'le Cokke'; the rent was in decay.[284] In 1442-3 there was mention of a place called the Greyhound, evidently owned by a member of the local gentry.[285] 'Le Lyonn' appears to have had facilities suitable for an establishment which offered accommodation and stabling, and may well have been the *hospicium* of that name listed in the North Quarter of Northampton in the 1503-4 rental.[286]

The 1503-4 rental named a number of inns (*hospicium*): the Crown, the Bell, the Tabard and the Bull in Swinewell Street; the Angel in Bridge Street; the Dolphin in Gold Street; the Lyonn in the North Quarter; the Harte which apparently stood somewhere near the Franciscan friary; and the Swan in the Drapery. A number of these establishments were located in areas of the town where there were gardens and much open ground. The rental made it clear that the owners included members of the local gentry, who perhaps grasped the commercial opportunities offered by a large townhouse with extensive accommodation and stabling. These houses may have followed a courtyard plan with four ranges around the courtyard; alternatively they may have consisted of a gatehouse with main rooms at the front and a courtyard to the rear.[287] The properties which were named as inns in 1503-4 featured in the late-thirteenth-century rental, but were not designated as inns at that

---

[283] BL, Add. Ch. 6057; Eg. Roll 2111.

[284] PRO, SC 12/3/39.

[285] *Early Chancery Proceedings*, vol. I, no. 16 on p. 54. Note also 'a place called the Tabard' (*ibid.*, no. 532 on p. 103).

[286] NRO, Royal Charter 29, m. 1d. It was held by the heirs of Richard Verney knight, and presumably the same as the 'place' occupied by a hosteler in 1452-65 (*Early Chancery Proceedings*, vol. I, bundle 27, no. 213).

[287] For discussion of the ground plans of early inns, see P. Clark, *The English Alehouse: a social history 1200-1830* (London, 1983), 6; M. Carlin, *Medieval Southwark* (London, 1996), 197-9.

date. Yet there was almost certainly more demand for their services in the earlier period. It therefore seems possible that at Northampton as at Winchester, commercial inns were not defined as such until the fifteenth century.

Archaeologists have identified a medieval inn near the centre of Northampton, at 34 Gold Street. This was a substantial property consisting of an entrance alley leading to buildings arranged around a central courtyard.[288] In the early modern period the site was known as 'The Goat'; possibly it had been called the Dolphin in the early sixteenth century, when it belonged to St James' Abbey. In the late-thirteenth-century rental a tavern (the only one listed) stood somewhere in the vicinity. In addition to the Dolphin, the 1503-4 rental listed a tenement with shops in Gold Street near the end of Woolmonger Street called the Cardinal Hat. The document is difficult to read at this point but the property does not appear to have been described as an inn. The Three Cups in St Peter's parish, and the Green Tree, the 'Catte' and the 'ffawkener' (all three near the Franciscan friary) were other named establishments listed in the 1503-4 rental which were not designated as inns. Possibly they were taverns, where wine was sold, or alehouses, which offered ale and basic accommodation to less affluent visitors. According to Henry Lee, writing almost two centuries later, Northampton's inns before the Dissolution were often 'very ordinary'; as a result travellers coming from the west were entertained by the abbot of St James', while the prior of St Andrew's offered hospitality to those coming from the north.[289] Even if this had indeed been the case, Northampton would nevertheless have been distinguished as a large town by the number of its inns.

---

[288] *Vide infra*, 39.

[289] *VCH, Northamptonshire*, vol. III, 58.

Civic buildings

From the earlier medieval period until the parliamentary Act of 1489 which reorganised borough government, St Giles' Church served as the meeting place for the town assembly. Meetings were held in the church itself, and elections took place in the churchyard. From 1381 at least, elections to parliament were also made there. It has been suggested that this venue had been chosen because it was equally remote both from the castle and from St Andrew's Priory.[290]

The earliest reference to the common hall dates from 1285, when the justices in eyre held their sessions for the borough *in communi aula.* This building was said to have been 'in a little close, adjoining the last house on the right hand in the lane going from the Mayorhold to the Scarlet well'. The town's 1385 charter recorded the guildhall (*gilda aula*) as the place where the mayor and bailiffs held their pleas, and in 1387 the guildhall was specified as the venue for sessions of the court of husting. It seems probable that by this time the civic authorities were installed on a different site, in the hall – 'apparently of fourteenth-century origin' – at the south-east corner of the Market Square, between Abington Street and Dickers Lane. In its original form the building was open at ground level, with the hall on the first floor. An additional storey was added later, perhaps in the fifteenth century. The reorganisation of civic government in 1489 may have proved the catalyst for this development.[291]

The reorganisation resulted from the recent 'greate divisions, dissentions and discordes' between the inhabitants 'of lytil substaunce and haveour' and those who were 'discrete, sadde and well disposed'. Similar discord had arisen in Leicester in

---

[290] *VCH, Northamptonshire*, vol. III, 8, 17, 57.

[291] *VCH, Northamptonshire*, vol. III, 36-7, together with drawing of building facing p. 34. For sessions of the court of husting in the guildhall in December 1378 and April 1422, see NRO, Royal Charter 28, m. 1; BL, Eg. Roll 2084.

1466 and 1467, when the unenfranchised evidently attempted to claim an equal share in elections with the burgesses. The ruling elite of both shire towns petitioned Parliament to support their vested interests; in response two acts were passed in the parliament of January-February 1489 which effectively placed the government of each town in the hands of a closed body.[292] Election day in Northampton thereafter began with mass in All Saints' Church, after which the mayor, ex-mayors, ex-bailiffs and 48 persons nominated by the mayor and his brethren proceeded to the guildhall to make their choice. This move from St Giles' Church may have prompted the building of an additional storey with battlemented parapet on the guildhall, although it has to be wondered how it was funded, especially if the townspeople were opposed. Possibly it was financed by the ruling oligarchy; if so, it is indicative of persisting wealth among the elite, and not of wealth in the civic coffers. No reference to the hall has been found in the wills, with the exception of that made by the weaver Richard Pakeman in 1493. He left his daughter four yards of woollen cloth that was in the town's common hall. This suggests that the hall had commercial functions, possibly connected with craft regulations.[293]

The fact that the hall was sometimes called the guildhall may indicate that some at least of the craft guilds may have used the hall for their meetings. This is not certain, since so little evidence for the late medieval companies survives. Moreover, it was claimed by Lee in 1715 that those companies which had constitutions regulating their trades used to meet in the hall over the great conduit, a building of two or three storeys erected in the market place in c.1481. This was possibly a replacement for the octagonal conduit, said to have been of fourteenth-century date, which stood at the south-west corner of All Saints' churchyard.

[292] *VCH, Northamptonshire*, vol. III, 9.

[293] Early Will Register, ff. 98r-98v.

Before the Dissolution, the shoemakers and shearmen apparently met at the Carmelite friary, and the fullers and slaters at Black Friars.[294]

The town had its own prison, first mentioned in 1253; the keys were in the custody of the bailiffs. In the sixteenth century it was described as adjoining the town hall, in Abington Street, but its earlier location is unknown. By 1586 the former open area below the hall had been filled in; eight shops now stood here and some rooms which would be used as prisons for about 200 years.[295] The cross in the market place was mentioned in deeds from the fourteenth and fifteenth centuries. It may have been destroyed in the fire of 1516, but was in any event replaced by a handsome new market cross in 1535. This was an eight-pillared construction with steps leading up into a lanthorne in which the market strikes and other equipment were kept. The lanthorne was well-glazed, the roof covered with lead and circled by statues of apes carrying little iron rods, and the whole was decorated with small pieces of lead gilded to resemble coats of arms. In 1535 a bequest of £67 towards making this cross was received from William Bownde, possibly the mayor of 1528-9. Small wonder that it was described as a 'great ornament' to the town.[296] The rental dating from the reign of Edward I listed several houses *Ad crucem Alnoth'*, which perhaps stood somewhere in the vicinity of Holy Sepulchre. This cross was mentioned in the 1332 rental of St James' Abbey (*vacuis placeis* paying rent of 6d).[297] In 1535 William Bownde left £10 to mending the highway in St James' End, beginning at the cross near Master Chauntrell's house.[298] Such crosses at the entrances to Northampton perhaps helped to emphasise the town's status. The

---

[294] *VCH, Northamptonshire*, vol. III, 25, 28, 51.

[295] *VCH, Northamptonshire*, vol. III, 20, 36.

[296] *VCH, Northamptonshire*, vol. III, 25; Serjeantson and Longden, 'Parish churches of Northamptonshire', 376. This cross was destroyed in the fire of 1675.

[297] PRO, SC 12/13/38; BL, Add. Ch. 6117. The cross was not named in the 1503-4 rental.

[298] Serjeantson and Longden, 'Parish churches of Northamptonshire', 376.

clock house which surmounted the chapel of St John by 1530 was another indicator of a large town.[299]

Paving, water supply and rubbish disposal

Archaeological excavations have identified evidence for road metalling in Northampton from the late eleventh and twelfth centuries, although the first substantial surfaces appear to date from the late middle ages. The date for substantial surfaces may perhaps be associated with the grant of pavage made by Edward I on 8 May 1285, to commence on the feast of St John the Baptist (24 June) and to last for two years. This grant in aid of paving the town enabled the civic authorities to take customs of 1d from (for example) carts carrying corn, fish and hides for sale; other goods on which customs could be levied included cloth, wine, wool, fleeces and sheepskins.[300]

No further grants of pavage are known. Perhaps the responsibility for paving devolved upon the urban community, although with what success is unclear. In 1431 the mayor and commonalty of Northampton petitioned for legal powers which would enable them to compel freeholders with tenements abutting the street to pave anew and afterwards whenever necessary to repair the pavement from the front of their messuage as far as the middle of the channel of the street, and in width from one corner of the messuage to the other. These powers were granted and were to apply to the following highways: from the North Gate to St Thomas' bridge, from the West Gate to the East Gate, and also Bearward Street, St Giles' Street, Kingswell Street, St Mary's Street, St Martin's Street and the way called the Market Place. Those townsmen with tenements abutting the market place could not be compelled to pave or repair the pavement further than 30 feet beyond the front

---

[299] Serjeantson and Longden, 'Parish churches of Northamptonshire', 372-3.
[300] *NBR*, vol. I, 54-5.

of their property. The rest of the market place was to be paved and repaired by the town.[301]

No references to amercements for failure to pave as required have been found in the surviving documentary evidence, and only three bequests for paving within the walls have been traced in the wills. In 1487 Thomas Whyte, parishioner of Holy Sepulchre, left 3s 4d to paving the Northgate; in 1500 his fellow parishioner Thomas Knight butcher left 12d to repair the highway between the church and the North Gate. In 1517, the year after the fire that allegedly consumed the greatest part of the town, William Saxby left £40 towards paving the market place 'so that the substantial men of the town will be bound by my executors to finish it up'.[302] This comment implies that private finance was available for the maintenance and repair of public amenities. Nevertheless, however financed, paved streets and market areas were clear indicators of a top-ranking town. In 1520-1 two pavers lived in the East Quarter of Northampton, and possibly obtained their stone from the quarry near the East Gate.[303]

The names Swinewell Street, Kingswell Street and Scarletwell Street indicate the presence of wells within the walls of medieval Northampton. The rental from the reign of Edward I listed a tenement near a well in Holy Sepulchre Street; a will of 1473 named a tenement next to the North Gate and opposite the well there.[304] A lease of 1499 related to a garden, dovehouse and pond in Knight Street.[305] The borough ordinances mentioned a fountain in the Cooks' Quarter (probably

---

[301] *NBR*, vol. I, 283-8.

[302] Early Will Register, f. 51r; PRO, PROB 11/14 4 Holgrave (f. 25v); Serjeantson and Longden, 'Parish churches of Northamptonshire', 377.

[303] NRO, Royal Charters 29, 31. 'Les delvys' next to the East Gate were mentioned in a will of 1488 (Early Will Register, f. 53v). Masons and hilliers are attested in this area (Royal Charters 29, 31).

[304] PRO, SC 12/13/38; Early Will Register, f. 11v.

[305] *Catalogue of Ancient Deeds*, vol. V, A 10945.

Mercers' Row).[306] It has been suggested that the tannery excavated north of Tanner Street and located some 400 feet from the river may have used well water.[307] The legal powers granted to the civic authorities in 1431 to enforce repairs to the pavements specified the channels in the streets as boundaries for the occupier's obligations. In 1520-1 five women living in the Chequer ward were each fined 8d for having washed *pannos lintheos* in front of their tenements in the high street.[308]

These references indicate relatively easy access to water within the town, with supplies perhaps boosted from elsewhere for the larger consumers, like the innholder Hugo Wodfall, whose will was witnessed by John Pewt'er alias Wat'man.[309] Martin le Waterleder was named as the former holder of a tenement in Swinewell Street in the rental of the reign of Edward I; the current occupier was then Juliana *a la ffuntaygne*. The rental of 1503-4 named him Martin Waterseller.[310] No other waterleaders have yet been found in the documentary sources. The situation in Northampton therefore contrasts with that at Leicester where the 'lochelmen called watermen' were sufficiently numerous to attract the attention of the authorities, who ordered them to serve the community faithfully and to refrain from forming an association.[311]

In August 1291 the Franciscans were licensed to unite the course of a spring called 'Triwell' running in three directions between the towns of Northampton and Thorp. The water was to be taken by a subterranean conduit to their house, and those persons with land in the field through which the conduit would be taken were to be

---

306 *NBR*, vol. I, 254.

307 Cherry, 'Leather', 296.

308 NRO, Royal Charter 30.

309 Early Will Register, f. 92v.

310 PRO, SC 12/13/38; NRO, Royal Charter 29.

311 M. Bateson (ed.), *Leicester Borough Records*, vol. II, 1327-1509, London (1901), 197. The date of this ordinance is uncertain but was possibly made in June 1383 .

indemnified for the damage, estimated at one mark, if their lands were sown at the time. In November 1292 St Andrew's Priory also sought to improve its water supply, and obtained permission to take spring water by an underground conduit over the land of Richard Gobion outside the town.[312] Evidence for similar arrangements to provide water for the urban community is later. An octagonal conduit at the south-west corner of the churchyard of All Saints' and taken down in 1831, is said to have dated from the fourteenth century. The 'great' conduit in the market place was erected c.1481, and was a building of two or three storeys, with a hall above the conduit in which companies with constitutions met to regulate trade.[313] This was perhaps the conduit mentioned in three wills of the early 1480s, made in the early years of its appearance.[314] Thereafter the townspeople perhaps took the conduit for granted. In the early sixteenth century, however, it needed repair, and the innholder John Adams made a bequest of 6s 8d for this purpose in 1509.[315] The concern of innholders for a good water supply is understandable.

The *Liber Custumarum Villae Norhamptoniae*, compiled in c.1460 but with later additions, indicated civic concern for hygiene. The town's dyers, butchers and other inhabitants were ordered not to throw into the highway 'grutte or dyzing of wod ne carione nor non other man'e stynkyng thyng'. In 1505-6 further ordinances were directed specifically to the butchers, who were forbidden from throwing any offal (lights, 'longis hornes' and other 'annoyable' things) behind their stalls or onto the pavements.[316] In every medieval urban community the

---

312 *Calendar of Patent Rolls* (1281-1292), 442, 511.

313 *VCH, Northamptonshire*, vol. III, 25, 51.

314 Early Will Register, ff. 29r (Agnes Clerke widow 1481), 36r (John Leynlie glover 1483), 38r (John Rychere innholder 1485). The plan of old Northampton, based on Speed's map and included in *NBR*, vol. II, end page of volume, marked the 'great Conduit' in the centre of the market place, and the head of the conduit to the east of the town, on the road towards Billing.

315 Serjeantson and Longden, 'Parish churches of Northamptonshire', 376.

316 *NBR*, vol. I, 229, 335.

authorities' efforts to force the inhabitants to clean the pavements before their doors, to keep drainage ditches scoured and to prevent pigs from roaming, were continuous but largely unavailing.[317] The limitations of their powers can be seen in the estreat rolls for Northampton's Chequer Ward and East Ward in 1520-1, which contained long lists of offences, including blocked or 'putrid' gutters, dung and old rushes thrown onto the pavements, and stockfish water and animal intestines discarded in the street.[318]

The rolls also contain an indication of some communal provision of refuse disposal facilities. Four muckhills are mentioned: 'Rokys muchill', 'Castell mukhill', 'Seynt pulcrez mukhill' and 'Seynt Gyles mukhill'. Possibly each served one quarter of the town, as did the four places designated for refuse disposal in Leicester in 1508.[319] Unlike Leicester, however, these muckhills appear to have been within the walls. For this reason perhaps, Northampton's ruling body showed concern for the type of rubbish that was deposited. Large numbers of townsmen and women were amerced for throwing *shreddes* and *scopis* on the muckhills; and one or two for using the muckhills as places to deposit dung. An entry in the first Stamford Hall Book indicates that similar concerns existed there. In July 1466 the governors of that town forbade the laying of 'stone, earth or timber, entrails or bowels or dead carrion' on the dunghills, nor indeed anything else but dung.[320] If urban dunghills or 'muckhills' were restricted to this use, with the dung presumably carted away to fertilise the town fields, then the question of the disposal of rubbish remains unanswered. There is no evidence at Northampton for

[317] For the distinctively 'urban' character of these problems, see G. Rosser, *Medieval Westminster, 1200-1540* (Oxford, 1989), 239-43.

[318] NRO, Royal Charters 30, 31.

[319] *Leicester Borough Records*, vol. II, 380. The places were all outside the walls: at the netherend of Belgravegate, in the field beyond Gallowtree gate end, beyond the Horse Fair and beside the Soar at the common privy.

[320] D.G. Teall, 'The Corporation and Tradesmen of Stamford 1461-1674', unpublished Ph. D. dissertation, University of Leicester (1975), 130.

the appointment of scavengers charged with carrying away refuse. Possibly communal rubbish disposal was financed, at least in part, by amercements levied in the annual views of frankpledge. The estreat rolls for 1520-1, resulting from the great view of frankpledge held in the guildhall before mayor and bailiffs, are the only such rolls to survive. The fines levied in Chequer Ward for that year amounted to £3 7s 1d, and in East Ward to £2 10s 0d. It cannot be assumed that the total was collected in full.

Town walls and gates

A town with a circuit of walls enclosing an intra-mural area of some 245 acres and with four main gates, each facing one of the points of the compass, clearly proclaimed its high ranking in the urban hierarchy of its region. Northampton's walls were mentioned in the borough charters of 1189 and 1200; murage grants, presumably for their repair, were made in 1224, 1251 and 1301. The 1224 grant was to last for three years, that of 1251 for two years, while the more extensive grant of 1301 was to last for five years, implying major work, possibly involving rebuilding rather than repair. An order to repair the walls, turrets and dykes was sent to the mayor and bailiffs in 1378, and in 1400 a further murage grant, for two years, was authorised.[321] The section of the wall between the East and North Gates had been in sufficiently good repair in 1278 for it to be used as a walkway, and it was still surmounted by battlements. The wording of the 1378 commission suggested that the whole circuit had subsequently been neglected, while the 1400 murage grant implied that restoration work was envisaged. By the sixteenth century, however, it seems that the whole circuit had been allowed to fall into disrepair. The town's walls only featured in the documentary sources as property

[321] *NBR*, vol. I, 36-7, 41-3, 58-60, 72-4; *VCH, Northamptonshire*, vol. III, 30; Williams, *Saxon and Medieval Northampton*, 38. He notes that the intra-mural area of Northampton was exceeded in England only by those of London and Norwich, and that it was roughly comparable with that of York.

boundaries, although this does suggest that they remained a significant feature of the urban landscape in the later medieval period.[322] A survey of St Andrew's Priory, made in 1538, listed a furlong 'next the wall of the village of St Edmund'.[323]

The gates of a medieval town served a variety of purposes. Locked at night, they provided a symbolic barrier between the urban and rural communities. They allowed access to the town to be controlled and non-resident traders to be taxed. They provided the setting for displays of civic pride and royal propaganda. Accommodation in buildings over the gates could be used to house the town prison or leased for commercial purposes.

Northampton's gates were mentioned in the reign of John, with the East Gate appearing to have then been the most important. This pre-eminence persisted into the seventeenth century, when the East Gate, dating like the other three from the fourteenth century, was described as being very handsome and adorned with coats of arms; the other three main gates were being used as tenements for the poor.[324] The importance of the East Gate is somewhat surprising, since the main road from London then approached the town from the south, using the river crossing (the South Bridge) established at or soon after the Conquest. In the middle ages roads from the East Gate led through St Edmund's End to Kettering and to Wellingborough. In the Anglo-Saxon period, however, the London road may have approached Northampton from the east.[325] A reflection of this earlier route may

---

[322] E.g., PRO, SC 12/13/38 (two tenements in St Giles' Street opposite the town wall, and two waste places next to the wall); NRO, Private Charter 48 (waste ground on west side of South Gate between town wall and ditch of running water); Royal Charter 29 (waste places in St Giles' Street next to the wall; waste tenement in St Peter's parish next to the wall towards the water).

[323] PRO, E 315/399, f. 266. Possibly the reference was to the town wall.

[324] *VCH, Northamptonshire*, vol. III, 30.

[325] Foard, 'Early Topography', 114, 119-20, with figure 2 on 111.

perhaps be glimpsed in the 1280 grant of a property in Abington Street (which led from the East Gate to the town centre) to a burgess on condition that he provided a kitchen and stabling for nine horses for London burellers during fair-time.[326]

The documentary sources have yielded no evidence for the collection of tolls at the town's gates in the medieval period, although fair and market tolls would have made an important contribution to the borough revenues. The only indication that the marketing activities of foreign traders were closely monitored comes in the 1520-1 estreat roll for the East Quarter, which included the names of butchers from Overston, Finedon and Castle Ashby who were amerced for *truncis* in the market place.[327] In the reign of Elizabeth traverse tolls were collected 'at the entrance to the town'. In c.1190 these tolls on animals and merchandise passing through Northampton were collected at certain fixed places; in 1329 it was claimed that since 1264 they had been collected along the roads leading to Northampton, in some cases at places as much as fifteen miles distant. In 1329 the toll places were at Slipton on the Kettering road, at Billing Bridge on the Wellingborough road, and at Syresham Cross on the Brackley road.[328] Northampton's attempts to exert its influence over such a wide area may be compared with similar attempts at Melton Mowbray. The Leicestershire town occupied a lower ranking in the urban hierarchy and in the fifteenth century the places at which passage tolls were collected were Saltgate in Kirby some 2-3 miles to the west of the town and Holwell mouth which lay a similar distance to the north.[329]

---

[326] *VCH, Northamptonshire*, vol. III, 24.

[327] NRO, Royal Charter 31.

[328] *VCH, Northamptonshire*, vol. III, 25.

[329] Melbourne Hall, Derbyshire, X94 Lothian, Box 34/4 (28 September 1440). Lord Ralph Kerr kindly gave access to the records at Melbourne Hall.

Functions

Northampton's central location ensured that the town played a strategic role of national significance in the early medieval period. Its position in the communications network helped the November fair to become one of the four great fairs of thirteenth-century England, at which royal purchases were made and at which payment for the king's prises from merchants was authorised.[330] In later years, as the town's military and political importance declined, it proved no longer necessary to maintain the castle as a major fortress. Northampton's fair also deteriorated, as did the other great fairs. All were losing ground by the end of the thirteenth century and their decline was complete by the first half of the fourteenth century.

Nevertheless, Northampton retained a number of functions that ensured that its top ranking in the urban hierarchy of its shire was maintained. It was the county town and the castle served as the administrative centre of Northamptonshire, as county gaol and as occasional royal residence, possibly during visits to the royal hunting lodges at Silverstone and King's Cliffe. Edward II stayed in the castle in 1307, 1308, 1310, 1311, 1317 and 1318.[331] Councils and parliaments were held at Northampton in 1307, 1328, 1336, 1338 and 1380. During the poll-tax parliament, however, the king stayed at Moulton and not at the castle, and the sessions took place in St Andrew's Priory.[332]

---

[330] *VCH, Northamptonshire*, vol. III, 24. Northampton purchases were paid for at the fair of St Ives, the St Ives purchases at Boston, the Boston purchases at Winchester and the Winchester purchases at Northampton. See also E. Miller and J. Hatcher, *Medieval England: Towns, Commerce and Crafts 1086-1348* (London, 1995), 166-7, 170-4.

[331] *VCH, Northamptonshire*, vol. III, 2 with n. 17.

[332] *NBR*, vol. I, 451; *VCH, Northamptonshire*, vol. III, 35.

An account of purveyance by the royal household during its sojourn in Northampton in the months of December 1300 and January 1301 gives an indication of the benefits the town derived from its presence. Three men supplied the household with bread to the value of £4 8d; 22 people (including one woman) supplied meat to the value of £59 3s 0d; 87 individuals supplied ale costing £35 14s 4¼d; wine costing £2 6s 8d was supplied by William le Somonour and by Robert de Toulouse. Robert de Bedford *apotecarius* of Northampton (who became mayor in 1304) provided wax and spices for the king's use costing £5 13s 9d. A further £10 5s 11d was spent on hay, litter, horse-shoes and nails. Other payments were made for mustard and fruit, and for assorted services such as baking, carpentry and carting, and for repairing barrels and horse harness. The total amounted to £196 16s 3d. On the dorse of the membrane a further 122 names were listed with the sum they were owed, together with 27 tallies from people whose names were not known. The downside to the king's presence was that it gave him the opportunity to recover debts due to himself, including £117 6s 8d for the fee farm and £20 arrears of a fine of 100 marks owing from the commonalty of the town for confirmation of its charters.[333]

The periodic presence of the justices and of the county sheriff brought local gentlemen to town. The great hall of the castle was made fit for the sessions of the justices in eyre who sat from November 1329 to May 1330; Northampton's mayor was ordered to supervise the preparations.[334] In May 1348 Thomas Bozoun of Woodford near Thrapston visited Northampton for the jousting one week, and the following week he was there for the forest eyre.[335] In August 1395 the knight

---

[333] BL, Add. Ch. 75994.

[334] *VCH, Northamptonshire*, vol. III, 34.

[335] G.H. Fowler, 'A Household Expense Roll, 1328', *English Historical Review*, 55 (1940), 630-4. The date has been corrected to 1348: C.M. Woolgar (ed.), *Household Accounts from Medieval England*, Part 2 (Records of Social and Economic History, New Series 18, published for the British Academy by Oxford University Press, 1993), 695.

Nicholas Lyllyng dated his acknowledgement of £5 received from the sheriff at Northampton; in October 1396 a number of Richard II's archers received their wages from the sheriff and they too dated their receipt at Northampton.[336]

Ecclesiastical visitors came on judicial business. In 1322 a group from Crowland Abbey stayed for several days while transacting business for the abbot. They paid for food and lodgings for themselves and their horses and took the opportunity to purchase a saddle.[337] In the early fifteenth century the prioress of Catesby (near Daventry) made the journey to Northampton when the malefactors who had broken into the priory, assaulted the servants and done considerable damage were brought to court. She was accompanied by a number of *generosi*, among them a member of the Catesby family, and the group spent £4 12s 0d during their visit, on wine, ale, fish and horse-bread.[338] The priory held property in the town. In 1428-9 this included a messuage in St Giles' Street called 'le Cokke'; 13s 8d rent was due from the convent property in 1448-9, of which 13s 4d was in decay. Thereafter the rentals only listed a garden, which produced no rent in the mid-fifteenth century.[339] This garden was in Swinewell Street and a rent of 16d was recorded in the 1503-4 rental. The Catesby family were near neighbours; the same rental listed William Catesby esquire as the tenant of two houses, a hall and a gate (*porta*) in St Giles' Street. Other gentlemen had similarly invested in town property, among them the knight Richard Verney, whose heirs in 1503-4 held a tenement in Holy Sepulchre Street and an inn called 'le Lyon' in the North Quarter.[340] Such investment is yet another indicator of Northampton's high ranking in the urban hierarchy.

---

[336] PRO, E 101/578/21; E 101/578/23.

[337] F.M. Page (ed.), *Wellingborough Manorial Accounts AD 1258-1323* (Northamptonshire Record Society, 8, 1935), 127.

[338] PRO, SC 6/947/4. No heading for this account roll survives, but it must be earlier than 1431 when Agnes Terry the prioress died.

[339] PRO, SC 12/3/29; SC 6/946/25; SC 6/947/2; SC 6/947/3.

[340] NRO, Royal Charter 29, mm. 1, 1d. William Catesby's house, hall and gate had formerly been held by Lord Zouche, for whom William Catesby II acted as officer in 1481: C.

The country gentry provided custom for the town's tailors as well as its victuallers. In the mid-1440s, when the town government imposed a constitution on the tailors, they emphasised the importance of the craft to the urban economy: 'Full many gentilmen and other people of oure lorde the Kynge for the shapyng of theire clothyng and of their servauntes and of theire lyveryeys dayly comen to the same town...'. These wealthy customers were often 'disseived' by 'unhable shapyng', to the detriment of the town, and ordinances for the craft were accordingly imposed by the mayor and burgesses.[341]

The gentry often had commercial interests of their own. In 1503-4, in addition to his property in St Giles' Street, William Catesby held two shambles on the north side of Butchers' Row. Richard Verney held a shamble (*scamella*) on the south side of the Row, and another in the Fishmongers' Row. These retail outlets were doubtless used for some of the meat and fish produced on their expanding estates. Many other gentlemen were named in this rental, holding shops in the Drapery for example, and inns and taverns throughout the town.

Northampton's ranking as a 'greater' town is indicated by the provision of sophisticated commercial and judicial services. The town possessed two seals for use under the Statute of Merchants for sealing recognizances: the great seal held by the mayor and the clerk's counterseal.[342] A list of the mayor's receipts for 1378-9 named thirteen men who each paid 6d for the statute seal or for a sealed certificate. Among them were Lord Ralph Bassett of Weldon, a merchant from Coventry, and

Carpenter, *Locality and polity: A study of Warwickshire landed society, 1401-1499* (Cambridge, 1992), 702. See this work for details of the Catesby and Verney families.

[341] *NBR*, vol. I, 265-7, 278-83.

[342] *VCH, Northamptonshire*, vol. III, 22. The design on the mayor's seal was like that for London, and the clerk's counterseal bore a representation of St Andrew on his cross. Names of those who held the counterseal can be found in the Patent Rolls: e.g., *Calendar of Patent Rolls* (1317-1321), 334; *ibid.* (1327-1330), 65; *ibid.* (1334-1338), 96, 256, 259; *ibid.* (1350-1354), 99, 518; *ibid.* (1364-1367), 15.

traders from Bedworth (north of Coventry), Daventry and Turvey in Bedfordshire.[343]

Judicial services included those provided by the ecclesiastical courts. For Northampton there is evidence only for their involvement in the granting of probate. In May 1435, for example, the will of Henry Caysho was proved in the church of All Saints' before John Lychebarwe, official of the archdeacon.[344] Wills of other local testators were proved in the church of St John's Hospital.[345] Wills provided work for scriveners like Roger Prynce, who was regularly named as a witness in the 1490s.[346] The notary William Mownford acted as witness and supervisor in the first decade of the sixteenth century.[347] A contemporary was the notary Richard Grene, a wealthy man who bequeathed his second-best gown of violet in grain with fur, his velvet tippet and velvet girdle decorated with silver to Master Thomas Knyght commissary of Northampton and his 'spiritual master'.[348] The presence of lawyers suggests that a town numbered among the larger urban communities. It must be added, however, that the legal profession was not prominent in Northampton in 1524-5. One scrivener was named in the first survey, and two in the second. Only one notary appeared, in the second survey, assessed on goods worth £45.[349]

---

[343] NRO, Royal Charter 28, m. 1d.

[344] BL, Add. Ch. 735.

[345] E.g., Early Will Register, ff. 6r, 7v, 11v, 81v, 82r.

[346] E.g., Early Will Register, ff. 99v, 100v, 102r, 103r, 104r, 106v, 111r. Prynce's own will, made in May 1498, suggests that his occupation was a relatively humble one; he left his son some bedding, a short gown of musterdevillers, 20s (if his debts allow) and 'God's blessing and mine': f. 117v.

[347] E.g., Early Will Register, ff. 124v, 129r, 133r, 133v, 142v, 145r, 153r, 184r, 188v.

[348] PRO, PROB 11/14 7 Holgrave (f. 49v). In the 1503-4 rental he was entitled 'Master' and held a house near the Franciscan friary; in his will he mentioned timber he owned in a 'lean-to' in the precinct.

[349] Dyer, 'Northampton in 1524', 79.

Northampton's role as marketing centre gave the town economic significance within the region. The charter of 1599 sanctioned the holding of a free market every Wednesday, Friday and Saturday by the burgesses 'as heretofore accustomed'. References to Saturday as market day can be found much earlier. Fourteenth-century meetings of the town assembly took place on all days except Saturday, the market day, and rarely on Mondays. In 1467 an ordinance for fishmongers ruled that it would be lawful for them to have stalls in the market place every Saturday in Lent; in 1520-1 a man was fined for regrating eggs and poultry at the market on a number of Saturdays.[350] In 1379 there was mention of butter purchased before the first hour on Friday in Easter week, which suggests that markets were also held on that day.[351] It would seem that market days in medieval Northampton were Wednesday, Friday and Saturday. Markets were held on the same three days at Leicester, with the Saturday market the most important commercially. Only the two shire towns had three market days, an indication of their ranking in the urban hierarchy. Possibly Saturday was the prime day for holding a market, and the larger towns would be anxious to have this as a market day.

There is no obvious documentary source that provides information about Northampton's markets. No records survive of the tolls collected (as at Melton Mowbray); nor are there any lists of revenues such as those from the butchers' stalls at Leicester for the year 1377-8.[352] Nevertheless, it is possible to draw upon various strands of evidence to gain an idea of the commodities traded and the geographical range of market contacts.

---

[350] *VCH, Northamptonshire*, vol. III, 8, 24; *NBR*, vol. I, 308; NRO, Royal Charter 31.

[351] NRO, Royal Charter 28, m. 1d.

[352] Melton Mowbray documents held at Melbourne Hall, Derbyshire; receipts from Leicester's butchers: LRO, BR III/8/9. An article on the market at Melton Mowbray is in preparation.

The market place adjacent to All Saints' Church had been created after the Conquest just outside the gate of the Anglo-Saxon *burh*. All Saints' was the major church of the new borough, and the market place was a central element in the town plan.[353] The names Sheep Street and Horsemarket suggest that in the medieval period livestock may have been sold elsewhere, as does the lost street name 'Nete Market'. Another lost name indicative of a separate location for the sale of a bulky commodity is 'le Strawechepyng'. The earliest citations given for these names in the Place-Name volume are late, but it would seem likely that the town had long provided a market for horses and livestock and for brushwood and straw.[354] The grant of murage in 1224 licensed the burgesses to take toll of ½d on every horse or mare, ox or cow taken to the town for sale, and ½d on every ten sheep, goats or pigs. The murage grant of 1252 mentioned these tolls, together with tolls on cartloads of brushwood, and on horseloads of brushwood and straw; similar tolls were recorded in the 1284 grant of pavage and the grants of murage in 1301 and in 1400.[355] In 1330 five prominent burgesses, including the serving bailiffs, were charged with taking unjust tolls throughout the year from all persons selling cattle, whereas nothing used to be taken out of fair-time, and then only from dealers and not from those who bought cattle for stock. They were also accused of extorting money from those who brought trusses of straw to sell to cover the 'Kingsbroth'.[356]

The murage and pavage grants listed other commodities which were brought to Northampton for sale. In 1252 these included trusses of cloth, cordulean leather,

---

[353] Foard, 'Early Topography', 115.

[354] J.E.B. Gower, A. Mawer and F.M. Stenton, *The Place-Names of Northamptonshire* (English Place-Name Society, vol. 10, 1933), 6-7. Dates given: Horsemarket (1545), Shepesmarket (1540), Netemarket (1540), 'le Strawechepyng' (fifteenth-century). A tenement in Shepcheping was listed in the 1332 rental of St James' Abbey (BL, Add. Ch. 6117).

[355] *NBR*, vol. I, 36-7, 41-3, 54-5, 58-60, 72-4.

[356] *NBR*, vol. I, 61-2. They were also charged with taking toll of 1d both from the vendor and the purchaser of an ox.

tanned hides from cattle and sheep, sea fish, salt, garlic, onions, flax, buckets, boards and millstones. These commodities were listed again in 1301, together with Aylsham linen, worsted cloth called coverlet, thin silk, wine, casks of sturgeon, horseloads of honey, tin, brass and copper, and every truss of whatever merchandise exceeding 10s in value. Included in the murage grant of 1400 were the same items, plus linen canvas cloth of Ireland, Galway worsted and Kendal, cloth of silk mixed with gold, samite, cendal, woad, madder, alum, oil of olives, Spanish wax, wax of Poland and Lubeck, steel goods and 'Aberdeen'.[357]

A section relating to the area around the market square is missing from the rental dating from the reign of Edward I. Nevertheless the document still provides a graphic depiction of the commercial heart of Northampton at that time, and shows that a number of Rows containing permanent shops had encroached upon the former open area. These Rows included the Row where wheat was sold, the Row where [ ] and dredge were sold, the Row opposite the Bakers, the Glovers' Row, the Mercers' Row, the Retailers' Row (*Rengum Regratorum Socorum*), the Butchers' Row, and the Drapery. No shops were recorded in the rows where corn was sold, and wheat and dredge may therefore have been sold from carts in the street. In the other rows, however, there were shops: at least fifteen in the Glovers' Row, at least eight in the Mercers' Row, and possibly fourteen in the Drapery. There were over fifty shops listed, excluding the butchers' shambles.[358] These were permanent retail premises, and on market days their number would have been greatly augmented by temporary stalls set up in the market place, and by countryfolk selling from baskets on the pavement.

---

[357] *NBR*, vol. I, 41-3, 58-60, 72-4. For the use of licences of murage, pontage and quayage as a rudimentary indication of the range of commodities which might be expected in a place (and the difficulties of the source) see C.M. Fraser, 'The Pattern of Trade in the North-East of England, 1265-1350', *Northern History*, 4 (1969), 45-6.

[358] PRO, SC 12/13/38; Williams, *Saxon and Medieval Northampton*, 41-2; RCHM, *Northampton*, 55-6.

In 1503-4, some sixty-five shops were listed in the central area. On the north side of Butchers' Row were twelve shambles and one shop; there were fourteen shambles on the south side. In Fishers' Row were twelve shambles and three shops.[359] Such a profusion of retail outlets could only be found in the largest towns. The shops of the earl in Leicester's market place in 1376 offered comparable provision: 88 in total rented by 13 shoemakers, 18 ironmongers, 23 drapers, 21 mercers and 13 butchers, who paid £11 8s 7d in rent.[360] The number of ironmongers in Leicester perhaps hints at a degree of specialisation, in a town which perhaps saw more metal-working than did Northampton. Few ironmongers are attested in Northampton: only one in 1524, for example, and three in 1525.[361] However, the will of the draper John Page in 1501 mentioned all the ironware in his shop in Northampton and at Daventry, suggesting that he dealt in commodities usually held by ironmongers. The draper William Rutter also stocked nails in his shop.[362]

A little information about those who brought merchandise into Northampton for sale can be gleaned from the *Liber Custumarum*. Goods brought by strangers included wool, hides, tallow, honey, cheese and meat; they were to be sold only in the 'kynges shoppe' and a 'comun shoppe' was also provided. Strange mercers, haberdashers, *cultellarii*, and sellers of hardware had been accustomed to stand with their merchandise on the usual market days 'especially between the fountain in the Cooks' Quarter (probably Mercers' Row since the Cooks' Arms stood by the conduit or fountain) and the west corner of the churchyard of All Saints'. This was proving inconvenient to passers-by and so the strange traders of whatsoever craft were ordered to stand on market days in the Hirelings' quarter near the fish stalls

---

[359] NRO, Royal Charter 29.

[360] *Records of the Borough of Leicester*, vol. II, 156.

[361] Dyer, 'Northampton in 1524', 77.

[362] Early Will Register, ff. 94v, 128r.

and not elsewhere. The *Liber Custumarum* also mentioned chapmen who sold their wares *de ostio ad ostium, loco ad locum, seu domo ad domum,* a practice which was of course prohibited. An ordinance of 1463 ordered foreign merchants and chapmen (such as drapers, mercers, hosiers, ironmongers, flaxmen and tanners) not to show their wares to the town's merchants and chapmen except 'within his inn'. This regulation did not apply to those who sold victuals.[363]

The murage grant of 1224 distinguished between carts and vehicles coming from Northamptonshire with saleable articles, and those which came from other counties; the former paid ½d and the latter paid 1d in toll. These differential rates indicate that some commodities were brought from beyond the county boundary and had perhaps travelled a considerable distance. Some commodities, however, and most notably victuals perhaps, were brought into the town by people who lived within closer geographical range. In 1378-9 the foreign butcher William Pateshull was amerced for buying meat before Prime in order to resell it. There is a strong possibility that he came from the village of Pattishall, some six miles to the south west.[364] Among those listed in the estreat roll of 1520-1 for the East Quarter were butchers from Overstone and Moulton (which lay some four to five miles to the north east), from Castle Ashby (c. seven miles to the east) and from Finedon, about thirteen miles distant. Each butcher was fined 3d for having a 'trunk' in the market which caused an obstruction.[365] Foreign butchers featured regularly in urban marketplaces. Several were named at Leicester in 1376, for example, and ordinances regulating their activities were included in Leicester's Hall Book. All butchers 'of the cuntray' who brought flesh to market were also to bring the skins and tallow; they were not to bring in any flesh which was 'corupte with eny maner

---

[363] *NBR*, vol. I, 221, 254-5, 264, 300-1. As noted above, the original document should be checked for the last reference.

[364] NRO, Royal Charter 28.

[365] NRO, Royal Charter 31.

of sekenes'; they were to keep their mares and horses out of the shambles.[366] Foreign butchers in Northampton who sold flesh in the '?kytestallis' were similarly ordered to bring with them the hides and tallow belonging to the flesh.[367]

Northampton's *Liber Custumarum* regulated the marketing activities of bakers, who were to sit together in a certain place in a particular Row. The same rules applied to the 'strange baxsters', among them men from Ecton, a small village some five miles north east of the town, on the road to Wellingborough. This was evidently a two-way trade. In 1467 Northampton's bakers were in trouble for selling bread of poor quality outside the franchise in 'diverse townships of the country'; and in 1518 there was mention of bread being loaded on horses and carried into the country and to the suburbs of St James' End, St Edmund's End and Cotton.[368]

There were also rules governing the sale of fish, an important element of diet in an age when the church ordained so many meatless days.[369] An ordinance for fishmongers in 1467 noted that there had been an accustomed place for all those selling sea fish, stock fish and other fish, but that people had been selling fish instead upon 'bakstalles' which had not been rented from the king. In future such fish was to be forfeited, with half the profits going to the town and half to the light in the 'high place afore the Rode' in All Saints' Church. It was to be lawful for stalls to be set up in the market place each Saturday in Lent.[370] In 1503-4 there were twelve shambles and three shops in the Fishers' Row, a sizeable number. At least six fishmongers served as bailiff between the years 1386-1461. William

---

[366] LRO, BR III/8/9; *Records of the Borough of Leicester*, vol. II, 288-9, 292.
[367] *NBR*, vol. I, 395.
[368] *NBR*, vol. I, 224, 309, 333.
[369] C. Dyer, *Standards of living in the later Middle Ages* (Cambridge, 1989), 58, 61-2, 197, 202.
[370] *NBR*, vol. I, 307-8.

Band, mayor in 1516-17 and 1528-9, may well have been the fishmonger William B[ ] who was assessed on goods valued at £95 in the subsidy of 1524 and thus the wealthiest townsman of his day.[371]

The River Nene flowed close to the western and southern walls of Northampton and this 'common water' was within the town's franchise and under the governance of chamberlains who paid 24s each year to the bailiffs in aid of the farm. In 1407 the river was said to be greatly denuded of fish, and orders were made governing the size of mesh and the size of fish caught; these orders applied to millers and to any who fished. Those who were enfranchised, however, were allowed to fish in the waters called 'old [?water]' , and to use 'shovenettes' each Wednesday, Friday, Saturday and on other fasting days. These were the days when fish was eaten, and also the days of Northampton's market. The sanctioning of the use of nets on these three days suggests that local fish may have been sold at the market.[372] Fish was also caught in the Nene at Abington; in 1423 the two watermills there and the associated 'fishings' were leased to three bakers of Northampton.[373]

Catches from more distant fisheries in this river and beyond also supplied the town's market. Regulations concerning the regrating of fish applied to an area within 24 miles of Northampton, and in 1490 there was mention of forestallers who journeyed sometimes by land and sometimes by water to intercept strange merchants bringing corn, fish, herrings and other items.[374] Fish featured

---

[371] PRO, E 179/155/124. Three fishers, assessed on goods valued at £25, £6 13s 4d and £6, were also listed, and one assessed on wages of 20s. The fishers were said to draw their catches from local ponds and rivers, while the fishmonger sold imported salt or dried fish (Dyer, 'Northampton in 1524', 75). William Band may well have been William Bounde who made his will in 1535 and included very generous bequests, among them £67 towards making the new cross in the market place (PRO, PROB 11/26 27 Hogen).

[372] *NBR*, vol. I, 258-60.

[373] *Catalogue of Ancient Deeds*, vol. III, C 3510.

[374] *NBR*, vol. I, 264, 320.

prominently among the commodities on which tolls were imposed in the murage grants. In 1252 there was mention of sea fish conveyed both by cart and on horses, and also of herrings, on which toll was paid at the rate of ½d per thousand. These may have reached the town by water. The grant certainly mentioned boats coming to the town laden with merchandise, including salt and corn.[375] There is evidence for medieval water transport on the Nene between Northampton and Yaxley in the earlier medieval period.[376] Yaxley was mentioned in the Peterborough sources exclusively in connection with fish; bream, tench, *dentriculos*, sturgeon, and especially herrings were purchased there. Other purchases of fish by Peterborough Abbey were made at Lynn. This port may have been the ultimate source of much of the sea fish that reached Northampton's market. The absence of references to Lynn in the Northampton sources is perhaps indicative of the intervention of middlemen.[377]

It should be noted, however, that John ffurbyssher of Norwich was named in the 1503-4 rental as the former holder of a *scamella* in Northampton's fishmarket, suggesting that supplies of sea fish could have come from Great Yarmouth, possibly via Stourbridge Fair where Peterborough Abbey bought fish and other merchandise.[378] This fair was much frequented by Northampton's merchants, with fish prominent among the commodities they purchased. In 1519 two of the king's justices of Common Pleas arbitrated in a dispute concerning the tolls to be paid by the freemen of Northampton to the town of Cambridge for 'fysshe and barrells and

---

[375] *NBR*, vol. I, 42-3. According to Miller and Hatcher it could be assumed in 1252 that Northampton would be provisioned with firewood and sea fish by boat: *Medieval England: Towns, Commerce and Crafts*, 144.

[376] J. Masschaele, *Peasants, Merchants and Markets: Inland Trade in Medieval England, 1150-1350* (London, 1997), 214-15.

[377] J. Greatrex (ed.), *Account Rolls of the Obedientiaries of Peterborough* (Northamptonshire Record Society, 33, 1983), 120, 142, 143, 145, 171, 181, 195 (Yaxley); 120, 143, 166, 181 (Lynn). Simon Draper of Lynn was named in the will of William May mercer in 1487 (Early Will Register, f. 50v).

[378] NRO, Royal Charter 29; *Peterborough Account Rolls*, 120, 180, 194-5.

all other stuffe and merchandyses by them particularly bought at Shyrebridge Feyre and all other manor of passages and carriages through and by the said town of Cambridge all times of year'. The mayor of Northampton was to pay 10s per annum in lieu of all tolls on goods of freemen provided that it should be lawful for the mayor and community of Cambridge to take 2d of every cart loaded with merchandise belonging to any freeman of Northampton going out of the said fair. Foreigners belonging to Northampton were to pay all customs and tolls due.[379]

The evidence thus suggests that a major source of sea fish in the late medieval period may well have been Stourbridge Fair, and that the fish was transported to Northampton by cart. In earlier years some fish may have been transported by boat. Perhaps Billing Bridge, at which through toll was demanded, saw some merchandise transferred from boats to carts.[380] In any event, it seems that supplies of sea fish came from eastern England, and this helps to explain why the town's fishers perhaps chose to congregate in the East Quarter. In 1486 Thomas Pounce fisher (who owned several hundred sheep) had lands in the fields outside the east wall next to the postern gate adjoining the churchyard of St Giles' Church; he bequeathed two sheep to Abington Church.[381] In 1520-1 the estreat roll for St Edmund's End and St Giles' parish listed four fishers whose offences included throwing stockfish water into the street in front of their tenements, washing salt fish twice, having two prices for barrels of herring, and mixing old oysters with fresh

---

379 NRO, Private Charter 56. Pinned to this indenture was an extract from the town books of Cambridge dated 9 January 1749 ordering the treasurer to wait on the mayor and corporation of Northampton to say that £8 was due for 16 years arrears. The 1675 fire caused such huge loss of property in Northampton because the town's traders had just restocked their shops at Stourbridge Fair (*VCH, Northamptonshire*, vol. III, 31). 'Stourbridge' coffers and spruce coffers were bequeathed by Northampton testators in the medieval period (e.g., Early Will Register, ff. 15r-16r, 82r, 111r, 154v).

380 *NBR*, vol. I, 222.

381 Early Will Register, ff. 44v-45r.

ones.[382] In the same year, but named in the estreat roll for Chequer Ward, William Pounce fisher (son of Thomas) was amerced for throwing rubbish on 'Seynt Pulcrez mukhil'. This indicates that he also lived in the eastern part of the town. The wealthy fishmonger William Bounde and the fisher William Bayly were amerced for having thrown fish water into the street; Bounde had also mixed black soap with white, and *filum cum coton*, while Bayly had sold barrels of herring at two prices. So too had the shearman Thomas Braynsford, who was also named in the St Giles' parish estreat roll for having thrown dung in Grope Lane. So he too apparently lived in the East Quarter, and was named in the Chequer Ward because he had committed offences in the market area.[383]

Fish sold at Northampton on which toll could be charged included salt mullet, hard fish, salmon, lampreys, sturgeon (named in 1301); the 1400 grant of murage listed fresh and salted salmon and lampreys, fresh and salted herrings and herrings of Scone, great and small stock fish.[384] The borough records indicate that mussels, eels and oysters were also available.[385] Fresh fish came from the local river, and perhaps from ponds on the estates of men like Richard Verney knight, who held a stall in Northampton's fishmarket in 1503-4. The feeding of carp in their ponds was a characteristic activity of lords in this period. Fishponds, probably of medieval origin, have been found at Abington, Dallington and Great Billing, and there is a well-preserved fishpond at Upton.[386] The watermill of St Andrew's Priory had an associated fishery in the river just beyond the precinct walls. In 1268 eighty bream were carried from King's Cliffe to the king at Northampton.[387] Much sea

---

382 NRO, Royal Charter 31. Among the four fishers were Thomas Wyllymot and William Noble who were assessed at £25 and £6 in the 1524 subsidy.

383 NRO, Royal Charter 30. Some fishers were also amerced for regrating eggs and poultry, and for selling ale without displaying the requisite sign.

384 *NBR*, vol. I, 59-60, 72-3.

385 NRO, Royal Charters 28, 30, 31.

386 RCHM, *Northampton*, 68.

387 PRO, E 315/399, ff. 254-69; *Calendar of Liberate Rolls* (1267-1272), 13.

fish came from the east coast, either from Lynn or Great Yarmouth, with actual purchases possibly made at Stourbridge Fair. Supplies were also obtained from London fishmongers.[388]

Northampton lay in an area of good pasture lands and there is no obvious source for the meat which reached the town's market. The surviving wills suggest that local butchers owned large flocks of sheep and few cattle, and that their connections stretched to the county boundaries, and perhaps particularly to the boundaries with Leicestershire and Warwickshire. The grazier Thomas Pepe, whose bequests in 1485 included over 200 sheep and three cows, left 20s to repair the church of Little Bowdon (near Market Harborough). In 1488 the butcher Edward Atwell referred to his tenement and pastures in the town and fields of Catthorpe and in the fields of Lilbourne, adjacent villages on either side of the Avon, the former in Leicestershire and the latter in Northamptonshire.[389] Welsh drovers may well have passed through these villages, en route from North Wales to Northampton and Buckingham, although many drovers opted for a more southerly route, through Kenilworth and Southam. Other drovers approached Northampton from the south west, along the ancient Banbury Lane which passed close to Rothersthorpe with Hunsbury Hill its original termination.[390] It is perhaps no coincidence that the Northampton butcher William Atwell had pasture grounds near to this route at Eastcote and left bequests to the church of Pattishall; nor that William Pateshull was named among the foreign butchers who sold meat in the

---

388 A London stock-fishmonger sued a Northampton man for debt in 1403; in 1424 a London fishmonger sued a Northampton tailor and a trader from Lynn sued a fishmonger from Northampton. These examples have been taken from the database of Common Plea debt cases kindly provided by Dr Jim Galloway of the Centre for Metropolitan History.

389 Early Will Register, ff. 39r, 91r-92r.

390 K.J. Bonser, *The Drovers, Who they were and where they went: an Epic of the English Countryside* (London, 1970), 193-5. The road on either side of Southam was known as 'Welsh Road'; during the spring and summer Welsh cattle were sold in districts around Northampton and Leicester, the heart of the grazing districts of the English plain.

town in 1378-9.[391] Occupations were rarely given for testators from towns other than Northampton in the Early Will Register; an exception was Nicholas Margitts, a butcher from Towcester who made his will in 1509.[392] In the valley of the Tove, some two miles north-west of Towcester, Sir Thomas Green in 1499 destroyed four houses and converted 200 acres of arable to pasture; by 1551 the lands were grazed by 2,000 sheep. The neighbouring hamlet of Caswell was eliminated in 1509, when the houses were destroyed and 300 acres enclosed and converted to pasture.[393] It seems possible that the Welshmen murdered at Northampton in 1329 while on their way to Bedford may have been involved in the cattle trade.[394] So too may have been the Warwickshire gentlemen William Catesby and Richard Verney who both held shambles in Northampton's Butchers' Row in 1503-4.[395]

Northampton's butchers owned large numbers of sheep, and may have been active in the wool trade. Edward Atwell junior referred to his wool house in the will he made in 1485.[396] The district surrounding Market Harborough may have been particularly suitable for grazing sheep. At the start of the sixteenth century a wealthy merchant stapler from Huntingdonshire owned a great deal of land in this area, both in Leicestershire and in Northamptonshire.[397] This regional specialisation perhaps explains the connections of the grazier Thomas Pepe with Little Bowdon. It should be noted, however, that in 1319 a man from Ashby St

---

391 Early Will Register, f. 40r; NRO, Royal Charter 28.

392 Early Will Register, f. 172v.

393 Steane, *Northamptonshire Landscape*, 171-3. The Catesby family of Ashby St Ledgers accumulated holdings at Watford in the fifteenth century; in 1485 they held 300 acres of arable land and 490 acres of pasture. Possibly stock destined for Northampton's market grazed here (*ibid.*, 173).

394 *Calendar of Patent Rolls* (1327-1330), 423.

395 NRO, Royal Charter 29.

396 Early Will Register, ff. 39r-40r.

397 Robert Boordon of Houghton: PRO, PROB 11/14 Holgrave (ff. 187-8). He left bequests to 22 churches, including those at Foxton, Gumley and Laughton in Leicestershire, and Braybrooke, Arthingworth, Clipston and Oxendon in Northamptonshire.

Ledgers undertook to deliver half a sack of good ewes' wool to a Northampton merchant. It therefore seems that there were many sources of wool.[398]

Little can be said about the sources of corn sold in Northampton's market. Wheat, oats, barley and dredge were routinely available, wheat sold in one Row, and the rest in a separate Row which was possibly close by. Both Rows may have been in the vicinity of the Franciscan friary.[399] The 1252 murage grant allowed toll of ½d to be taken from every cart bringing corn for sale, and toll of ¼d from every quarter of corn conveyed by water. By the time of the pavage grant of 1284 the toll on cartloads of corn had been doubled, and there was no mention of corn conveyed by water.[400] It seems probable that corn was brought from many settlements, wherever a surplus was available, as too perhaps were supplies of hay and fodder. In 1281 carrying services to Northampton from Kettering, some fifteen miles distant, applied to these last two commodities.[401]

Demand for animal hides in Northampton had apparently been strong from an early date. The 1252 murage grant imposed tolls on tanned hides of horses, mares, oxen and cows, and also on tanned sheepskins. The 1284 pavage grant listed hides which were fresh, salted or tanned.[402] Some of these hides would have been brought to the town by foreign butchers, by order of the civic authorities, who refused them permission to sell meat in Northampton unless they did indeed bring the hides and tallow belonging to the flesh.[403] There is occasional evidence for other sources of hides. In 1453-4, for example, John Ashborne of Northampton

---

398 *Catalogue of Ancient Deeds*, vol. IV, A 9616.

399 PRO, SC 12/13/38; NRO, Royal Charter 29.

400 *NBR*, vol. I, 42, 55.

401 BL, Add. Ch. 737.

402 *NBR*, vol. I, 42, 55.

403 *NBR*, vol. I, 395. The same rules applied at Leicester and Exeter (*LBR*, vol. II, 288-9; Kowaleski, *Local Markets and Regional Trade*, 300). They were probably common in many medieval towns.

purchased 34 sheepskins from Catesby Priory; and in 1463-4 it seems that Simon ffysher of Northampton and his associates may have paid a fine of 1s for an annual licence to buy sheepskins at Melton Mowbray.[404] Hides may also have been purchased (and sold) at fairs. The town's butchers were in fact forbidden from taking fresh hides out of the town to sell anywhere else but at fairs.[405]

The thirteenth-century murage and pavage grants allowed tolls to be levied on animals taken to Northampton for sale: on horses, mares, oxen, cows, sheep, goats and pigs. This livestock market is reflected in names recorded in the medieval period such as 'Shepcheping', *forum porcorum* and 'Nete Markett', and in the surviving street names Sheep Street, Horsemarket and Marefair.[406] The animals sold presumably came from the rural hinterland and from elsewhere in the shire and beyond; some of them perhaps originated in Wales. In 1392-3 a horse belonging to John Catesby of Ashby St Ledgers was sold at Northampton, an indication that the town's later reputation as a centre for the purchase of horses had perhaps been founded in the medieval period.[407]

In the reigns of John and of Henry III considerable purchases of cloth for the royal household were made at Northampton's fair. The town's textile workers doubtless produced much of this cloth, but some would have been manufactured elsewhere. The thirteenth-century murage and pavage grants sanctioned the levying of toll on cloth carried to Northampton either on horseback or on carts. The 1301 grant mentioned worsted, worsted called 'coverlet', linen of Aylsham and thin silk; the 1400 grant referred to linen canvas cloth of Ireland, Galway worsted and Kendal,

---

404 PRO, SC 6/947/2; Melbourne Hall, X94 Lothian, Box 34/5, 1463-4.

405 *NBR*, vol. I, 227.

406 BL, Add. Ch. 6117; PRO, SC 6/948/18; *Place-Names of Northamptonshire*, 7.

407 PRO, E 101/51/15 (noted in a transcript kindly provided by Professor Christopher Dyer); *VCH, Northamptonshire*, vol. III, 29.

samite, cendal, and cloth of silk mixed with gold.[408] Woollen cloth would have been sold in the Drapery, and the linen and expensive silks in the Mercers' Row. Involvement in this trade required capital and Northampton's drapers and mercers always numbered among the town's leading men and dominated civic government. In the years 1386-1461 (when the lists of mayors and bailiffs in many instances included occupations) at least 19 mercers and 11 drapers served as bailiff, and in the years 1387-1459 at least 11 drapers and 8 mercers held the mayoralty.[409]

The trading networks of these wealthy merchants were necessarily extensive. The mercer John Bykerston (who made his will in 1467) had a brother-in-law in Taunton who was also a mercer. The draper William Rushden (whose will dates from 1466) had a relative in Stratford. In 1487 Simon Draper of Lynn was named in the will of the mercer William May; among the beneficiaries of the clothier Thomas Whyte in the same year was a namesake at St Alban's. In 1494 the draper William Prentese left his lands and tenements in Bloxham (Oxfordshire) to his son.[410]

There is evidence that indicates commercial links with London. By the late medieval period London's commercial dominance over the provinces was firmly established and the capital's pre-eminent position in the distributive network was assured.[411] The historical sources suggest that Northampton (like other East Midland towns such as Leicester and Melton Mowbray) looked to London for expensive imports and luxury items. In 1490 'London sheets' were listed among the goods of a Northampton innholder, and in 1502 the widow Alice Cutberd left her daughter 'my gown of puke that came from London'.[412] Provincial merchants

---

[408] *NBR*, vol. I, 42, 55, 59-60, 73-4.

[409] *NBR*, vol. II, 549-50, 556-8.

[410] Early Will Register, ff. 1v, 6r, 50v, 51v, 102v-103r.

[411] D. Keene, 'Medieval London and Its Region', *The London Journal*, 14 (1989), 105-6.

[412] Early Will Register, ff. 92r, 152v.

regularly travelled to the capital to make their purchases, as is evidenced by debt cases heard in the court of Common Pleas. London mercers, drapers and grocers sued Northampton traders in 1384, 1403 and 1424.[413] There is also evidence for the presence of Londoners in Northampton. In 1455 the London mercers Hugh Wych and William Sewster held a shop with chambers and houses 'above builded' in the Old Drapery, which they leased to a Northampton mercer. In the same year Hugh Wych, in association with two Cestrian mercers, was granted a messuage with a cellar and two shops in the commercial heart of Chester, at the corner of Bridge Street and of Watergate Street.[414] Hugh Wych was of Cheshire origin and it may be that the long-distance linkages indicated by these property holdings demonstrate a linear connection joining the capital to other market areas.[415]

London merchants supplied at least some of the wine bought and sold in Northampton. In 1378-9 a townsman was amerced 30s for acting as mainpernor for a Londoner selling wine without licence from the mayor. In 1384 a London vintner sued a Northampton man for £13; in 1403 a second vintner from the capital appeared as plaintiff attempting to recover £4 from John Wedon of Northampton. And in 1529-32 a local innholder owed money for wine purchased from a London grocer.[416] Few vintners are attested in Northampton in the later medieval period.

---

413 E.g., in 1384 John Maymond mercer v William Bras (debt of £24); Simon Worsted mercer v Agnes Worsted (debt of £2); in 1424 Alan Everard mercer v John Clerk chapman (£7 10s +), v John Wemmes chapman (£5) and v Richard Wemmes chapman (£5). Richard Wemmes apothecary was bailiff of Northampton in 1408 (Common Pleas database).

414 *Catalogue of Ancient Deeds*, vol. III, A 7651; Chester City Record Office, MR 96, m.1. Hugh Wych also did business with a chapman from York, to whom he had doubtless sold some of the Brabantine and Champagne cloth, lawn, fustian, canvas and buckram listed in the chapman's inventory of 1446: P. Nightingale, *A Medieval Mercantile Community: The Grocers' Company & the Politics & Trade of London 1000-1485* (London, 1995), 440.

415 S. Thrupp, *The Merchant Class of Medieval London* (Ann Arbor, University of Michigan, 1989), 375-6; J. Laughton, 'Aspects of the social and economic history of late medieval Chester, 1350-c.1500' (Ph.D. thesis, University of Cambridge, 1994), 246-7.

416 NRO, Royal Charter 28; Common Pleas database; *Early Chancery Proceedings*, vol. VI, Bundle 636, no. 55.

William Hogge, bailiff in 1453-4, is the only vintner known to have held high civic office. Just one vintner is recorded in the Early Will Register: John Barre, who witnessed the will of the innholder William Multon in 1485.[417] No vintners were listed in the 1524-5 subsidy surveys.

Grocers too are absent from the sources, apart from two named in the 1524 subsidy, one of them the third wealthiest townsman at that time with goods valued at £60. One grocer was listed in the subsidy of the following year, with goods worth £40.[418] Possibly there had been changes in the vocabulary of trade designations, as had happened in Winchester, with grocers being known earlier as spicers; this change may have been influenced by the prevailing London usage.[419] It is possible that demand for the commodities traditionally handled by grocers was not sufficiently strong at Northampton in the later medieval period to warrant specialist merchants. The town's mercers, drapers and ironmongers may have dealt in these wares, for they would have had the commercial contacts and the necessary capital.

Northampton's dyers also established contacts beyond the region in order to obtain the dyestuffs necessary for their trade. It seems that some supplies may have been

---

[417] Early Will Register, f. 41v.

[418] PRO, E 179/155/124; Dyer, 'Northampton in 1524', 77.

[419] Keene, *Winchester in the Later Middle Ages*, vol. I, 250-1; *idem*, 'Medieval London and its Region', 105. The spicer William Darby, who served as bailiff of Northampton in 1442-3, is the only recorded example of this trade. At Winchester the titles *apotecarius* and *speciarius* were synonymous in the thirteenth century; the term 'apothecary' was not used from c.1350 until the mid-fifteenth century, when it denoted a trader similar to the modern pharmacist. There are hints that Northampton may have witnessed a similar change in terminology. In 1300-1 Robert de Bedford *apotecarius* provided spices for the royal household during its stay in Northampton (BL, Add. Ch. 75994). In 1421-2 the apothecary Richard Wemmes served as mayor of the town; in the court of Common Pleas in 1424, however, he was described as 'chapman'. The apothecary Henry Baldeswell was bailiff in 1440-1; in 1455, however, when he leased shops and chambers in the Old Drapery from two Londoners, he was described as a mercer. Two apothecaries were named in the 1524-5 subsidies: William Fisher with goods valued at £13 6s 8d, and John Spencer, assessed on goods worth £4. Neither featured among the wealthiest townsmen, although Fisher was bailiff in 1528-9.

purchased from Londoners. In 1424 the London grocer William Wetenhale sued two Northampton dyers for debt.[420] As noted above, however, Northampton appeared in the Brokage Books of Southampton in the 1460s and 1470s as an important destination for dyestuffs, although demand for woad was always far greater in Coventry.[421] It is possible that Coventry acted as a distributive centre for dyestuffs (some perhaps from Bristol) and that Northampton dyers purchased some supplies from its traders.[422] In 1395, for example, the dyer John Ratford acknowledged a debt of £5 to a Coventry merchant.[423]

Four Northampton burgesses were members of Coventry's Trinity Guild. The two surnamed 'Corviser' perhaps travelled regularly to Coventry to obtain animal hides. The fuller John Chirche and his wife were also members.[424] Chirche had joined the guild in the mid-1420s, paying an admission fee of 10 marks and 5s; he possibly looked to Coventry as a finishing centre for his cloth. The advantages of membership grew clear when, in his eighties, he became enfeebled and unable to work and thus 'likely to perish for want of sustenance'. A petition to the guild wardens in 1453 from Northampton's mayor resulted in the grant of a yearly allowance of 26s 8d.[425] Links between Northampton's textile workers and Wellingborough are also attested. The dyer William Mylle had lands and tenements in that town in 1492, as too did his contemporary the weaver Richard Pakeman. Some of this latter property was in the tenure of a fuller, which raises the possibility that some cloth woven in Northampton was fulled at

[420] Common Pleas database; Thrupp, *Merchant Class of Medieval London*, 373-4.

[421] Colman, *Brokage Books of Southampton*, xxxiv, 323, 324.

[422] Phythian-Adams, *Desolation*, 20.

[423] A. Beardwood (ed.), *The Statute Merchant Roll of Coventry 1392-1416* (Dugdale Society, 17, 1939), 16.

[424] M.D. Harris (ed.), *The Register of the Guild of the Holy Trinity, St Mary, St John the Baptist and St Katherine of Coventry* (Dugdale Society, 13, 1935), 4, 40, 45, 64.

[425] L. Fox, 'The Administration of Gild Property in Coventry in the Fifteenth Century', *English Historical Review*, 55 (1940), 641.

Wellingborough, and/or that cloth fulled there was brought to Northampton to be dyed.[426]

Facilities for fulling cloth were of course available closer to the county town, at the fulling mills owned by St James' Abbey at Billing and at Cotton Marsh. There was a tenter-yard on the open ground south of the town wall near Mervyn's Mill. At some point in the second half of the fifteenth century it had been held by a Londoner but by 1481 it was held by the Northampton fuller Nicholas Bowker.[427] There is a little evidence for weaving being carried out at Kingsthorpe. In 1498 the weaver Roger ffauke of Kingsthorpe left a linen loom and two linen gears to his servant, and other linen and kersey gears to a man from Brafield. The Northampton draper John Page in his will of 1501 mentioned much property in Kingsthorpe, including a 'garett house'; a weaver and a shearman witnessed this will.[428] It is possible that such contacts linked country dwellers of the immediate hinterland with the town, and helped to determine the social and commercial networks which developed.

The late medieval documentary sources for Northampton hint at the attractive draw of London for the town's wealthier men, although the nature of their contacts can rarely be determined. Northampton burgesses held land in Dunstable, for example, and purchased lands elsewhere in Bedfordshire and Buckinghamshire; they had

---

[426] Early Will Register, ff. 95r-95v, 98r-98v. The fulling mill at Wellingborough yielded 13s 4d per annum in the 1290s and in the first decade of the fourteenth century; in 1312, 1314 and 1322 (when it was leased at farm) it yielded 16s (*Wellingborough Manorial Accounts*, 74-5, 79, 84, 89, 94, 98, 103, 107, 112, 117, 122). It was leased for 13s 4d in 1482-3 (BL, Eg. Roll 8440).

[427] N.R.O, Royal Charter 29; Early Will Register, f. 30v. The 'long curtilage' next to the mill was listed in the rental from the reign of Edward I but no usage was specified (PRO, SC 12/13/38).

[428] Early Will Register, ff. 62r, 128r.

links with Stratford (possibly Stony Stratford), Newport Pagnell, and St Albans.[429] Wills proved in the Prerogative Court of Canterbury included those of testators with interests in London, Buckinghamshire and Bedfordshire.[430] London plaintiffs who sued Northampton traders in the court of Common Pleas in 1384, 1403 and 1424 included vintners, mercers, fishmongers, a grocer, an ironmonger, and a shoemaker.[431] As noted above, two London mercers leased property in the Old Drapery in 1455 and a Londoner held the tenter-yard near Mervyn's mill for a period in the second half of the fifteenth century. In 1503-4 Nicholas Bultesham of London held a capital tenement in St Giles' Street and William Bray of London held a tenement in Bridge Street. Londoners possibly acquired property interests in Northampton through inheritance as well as through commercial interests.

Customers of Northampton's market and shops

The nearest markets to Northampton which functioned throughout the medieval period and beyond were Towcester, Daventry and Wellingborough, all of which were at least ten miles distant. The markets of Long Buckby, Brixworth and Wollaston, all functioning in 1330 but not in the sixteenth century, were nearer, but they were held on Tuesdays and thus did not clash with Northampton's market days.[432] The county town therefore enjoyed unrivalled pre-eminence as marketing

---

429 *Catalogue of Ancient Deeds*, vol. I, C 1606; Early Will Register, ff. 6r, 51v, 99r, 133r. These land holdings followed the line of the major route from London to Northampton and the north depicted on the Gough Map.

430 E.g., Thomas Swyfte (1492) with interests in London and Northampton (PRO, PROB 11/9 18 Dogett); John Chauntrell (1509) with interests in London and Northampton (PROB 11/16 24 Bennett); William Elmes (1504) with interests in London, Stamford, Northampton and Buckinghamshire (PROB 11/14 11 Holgrave); Thomas Astry (1518) with interests in London, Buckinghamshire, Hertfordshire, Northampton and Oxford (PROB 11/19 10 Ayloffe).

431 Common Pleas database.

432 Peter Goodfellow, 'Medieval Markets in Northamptonshire', *Northamptonshire Past and Present*, 7 (1987-8), 305-23; James Masschaele, 'The multiplicity of medieval markets reconsidered', *Journal of Historical Geography*, 20 (1994), 255-71.

centre for the rural hinterland. The town's fairs remained important, although their early medieval prominence had declined; these would have drawn customers from further afield. In 1286 Leicester Abbey spent 65s 6d at Northampton's fair, purchasing a laver (*lavatorium*) and a basin for use in the infirmary, three and a half ells of canvas, three lambskins for the abbot, and some spices. The expenses of the cellarer amounted to 25s.[433] In 1404-5 Peterborough Abbey purchased cloth to the value of £14 9s 10d at Northampton and the carriage to Peterborough cost 2s. More cloth was purchased in 1414, when the two abbey servants sent to buy it received 3s 5d in expenses.[434]

The nature of the contact which led Northampton plaintiffs to sue in the court of Common Pleas in 1384, 1403 and 1424 is not revealed in the records. The debt cases do attest, however, links between these men and townsmen from elsewhere, for example between one of the town's glovers and a resident of Oxford, between Simon Spycer of Northampton and Thomas Deyster of Daventry, between a Northampton draper and William Draper of Oundle, and between one of the town's tanners and a shoemaker from Olney in Buckinghamshire.[435] It is possible, therefore, that traders from the larger marketing centre sold goods to petty traders from smaller places. Such a connection may explain the character of the association attested between the Northampton draper William Rutter and William Russell of Daventry. It is clear from the will he made in 1491 that Rutter was also

---

[433] PRO, SC 6/1257/12. In the same year the abbey spent £37 12s 9d at Stamford fair, and £133 17s 6½d at the fair at Boston. For discussion of the abbey's use of fairs and local markets, see R.H. Hilton, *The Economic Development of some Leicestershire Estates in the fourteenth and fifteenth Centuries* (London, 1947), 29-33.

[434] *Account Rolls of the Obedientiaries of Peterborough*, 117, 144-5. The accounts did not specify that the purchases were made at the fair, but it is clear that they were made on a single occasion and this suggests that the fair was the occasion for the purchases. Purchases included black cloth and violet cloth, 'Ray' for the paupers in the hospital, coloured cloth *pro vadlettis et garcionibus pro liberacione estivale*, 1½ dozen of 'motley' *pro armigeris*, and other 'motley' for the *garçionibus*.

[435] Common Pleas database.

involved in the ironmongers' trade; goods in his shop included iron, steel, 'osmondes', and considerable quantities of nails.[436] The account rolls of Catesby Priory frequently recorded purchases of ironware and of nails from the ironmonger William Russell of Daventry in the mid-fifteenth century.[437] It seems that Russell (or perhaps his son) obtained his stock from Rutter, and that a close social relationship developed between the two men. This was reflected in Rutter's will, which included generous bequests to William Russell himself, and to his wife and to his son, also named William.

Catesby Priory did not purchase ironware at Northampton, although the nuns certainly looked to that town for some commodities. Horse traces and ropes for agricultural purposes were regularly purchased from a roper in St James' End; wax, spices, currants and paper were obtained from Northampton traders. In 1448 twelve dishes and a bowl were bought in the town, and in 1453-4 a saddle and bridle were purchased from Richard Goselyng of Northampton.[438] For ironware, however, the priory evidently preferred to deal with a more local man, perhaps because this may have lessened the transport costs of heavy items. Supplies of iron, incidentally, may have been obtained even closer to home for this reason. In 1453-4, for example, the priory bought 50 lbs of Spanish iron from a smith at Staverton, just two miles distant.[439] There may have been a difference in quality in the ironware available in smaller and larger centres. In 1453-4, when a new hall was built at Catesby, 9,000 stone nails and 400 board nails were purchased from William Russell of Daventry, but a Warwick trader provided the iron handles and hinges for the doors and windows.[440]

---

[436] Early Will Register, ff. 94r-94v.

[437] E.g., PRO, SC 6/946/21 (1448), SC 6/947/1 (1453-4). Russell supplied the priory with canvas and packthread, which he could also have obtained from Rutter.

[438] PRO, SC 6/946/21; SC 6/946/22; SC 6/946/24; SC 6/947/1. The saddler Richard Goslyn was bailiff in 1429-30.

[439] PRO, SC 6/947/1.

[440] PRO, SC 6/947/1.

The purchase of cloth at Northampton's fair has been noted above. It seems that the town was also viewed as a centre where well-made clothes were available. The importance of the tailors' craft to the urban economy was stressed in the constitution imposed upon those craftsmen in 1444-5, in which reference was made to the long tradition of the king's gentlemen and other people coming to Northampton for their own and their servants' clothes. An indication of the truth of this assertion can be seen in the will made in 1410 by a canon of Lincoln; he left to his brother the jacket and doublet he had bought from William Begworth of Northampton.[441] By the 1440s, however, this business was being prejudiced by bad workmanship, and the town government accordingly decreed that two wardens be appointed to oversee the craft and a hall provided in which meetings could be held.[442] Twenty tailors were named in the subsidy of 1524, and seventeen in the subsidy of 1525, making them one of the largest occupational groupings. In 1524 ten tailors were assessed on wages, two of them receiving above average wages of £2 and 26s 8d. Ten tailors were assessed on goods, the wealthiest of them on goods valued at £13; he became bailiff in 1527.[443] Five tailors were named in the estreat roll for Chequer Ward in 1520-1, and one in the estreat roll for East Ward. Two of these tailors were amerced for having sold cloth *non adaquat'*.[444]

Population and wealth

In 1086 Northampton contained 47 burgages, 14 'mansions' that were now waste, plus 40 burgages in the new town in the king's demesne. It also contained 219 other houses owned by 34 different lords, making a total of some 306

---

[441] A. Gibbons, *Early Lincoln Wills 1280-1547* (Lincoln, 1888), 123. Begworth served as bailiff in 1397-8.

[442] *NBR*, vol. I, 265-6, 278-83.

[443] PRO, E 179/155/124; Dyer, 'Northampton in 1524', 76, 79. The other tailors assessed on goods in 1524 had goods valued at £6, £4 (2), £3 (2) and £2 (4).

[444] NRO, Royal Charters 30, 31.

householders. A figure of between 291 and 301 houses and 36 waste plots has been given, from which a population of 1,032 has been suggested. This figure has been queried and a total nearer to 1,500 considered more likely. The farm of the town was set at £30 10s 0d, which was roughly comparable with (for example) Derby, Nottingham, Torksey and Worcester. Northampton lay between 20th and 30th in a ranking based on farms.[445]

By 1130-1 the farm had more than trebled to £100, and it was raised to £120 in 1184. This was exceeded only by London, Lincoln, Winchester and Dunwich. The aids and tallages rendered to the king in the years 1158-1214 provide further proof of Northampton's prosperity in that period. The town never fell below seventh in these rankings; in 1172 it was third to London and Lincoln and in 1176/7 it was second to London. In 1194 Northampton's Jewry ranked fifth in England, and in 1202, when Leicester, Winchester and Northampton paid £10 to be free of the assize of cloth, only York, Lincoln and Beverley paid more.[446] The town's intra-mural area of some 245 acres (100 hectares) was exceeded only at London and Norwich. In 1746, when the town was confined within the walls and when the area included large open spaces, the population stood at 5,136. It is unlikely that the twelfth-century population was smaller, unless a rural area had been enclosed as a speculative venture to attract settlers. It has been estimated that Winchester, a town of comparable wealth at this time, had a population in excess of 8,000 in the mid-twelfth century.[447] Moreover, Northampton had experienced large-scale suburban development by this same period. It has been estimated that

---

[445] *VCH, Northamptonshire,* vol. III, 2; RCHM, *Northampton,* 47. A figure of 330 houses, of which no less than 100 belonged to the king, has also been quoted; presumably the 'waste' property was included in this total (*NBR*, vol. I, xvii).

[446] RCHM, *Northampton,* 47, 48; *VCH, Northamptonshire,* vol. III, 27. There were 112 Jews in London, 82 in Lincoln, 42 in Norwich, 40 in Gloucester and 39 in Northampton.

[447] RCHM, *Northampton,* 51-2. In c.1300 the population of Winchester was between 10,000 and 12,000, and may have been at least as great as this in the twelfth century (Keene, *Winchester in the Later Middle Ages,* vol. I, 368).

by 1300 the suburbs covered an area more than half the size of the walled town itself.[448]

The burgesses appear to have experienced difficulty in paying the fee farm at the beginning of the reign of Henry III. Their arrears in 1227 were such that the town was taken into the king's hands and a *custos* appointed.[449] Yet Northampton remained a flourishing urban centre and thus attracted the Franciscan and Dominican friars soon after their arrival in England. Both orders established important houses in the town in c.1230, and the Carmelites and the Friars of the Sack settled there within the next fifty years. The Augustinian friars founded a house either in the late thirteenth century or in 1323.[450] In 1264 Northampton, which had been held by the younger Simon de Montfort and a 'great multitude' of knights and squires, was captured by the king's troops and ruthlessly sacked. It was said that they reduced a most prosperous town to a most wretched state. The mayor was again removed and a *custos* appointed.[451] Northampton's decline was apparent ten years later, when the lesser folk complained that they bore the burden of tallages and other charges, and that as a result many craftsmen had left. The population at this time was possibly about 3,000, a considerable reduction from that of the late twelfth century.[452] This figure is suggested by the royal rental dating from the reign of Edward I which recorded about 300 properties. The section relating to the area around the market square is missing, and an additional 69 properties were listed in this area in the subsequent rental of 1503-4.[453] Also

[448] Foard, 'Early Topography', 120-1.

[449] *VCH, Northamptonshire*, vol. III, 19.

[450] RCHM, *Northampton*, 55; *VCH, Northamptonshire*, vol. III, 58-9.

[451] *VCH, Northamptonshire*, vol. III, 3.

[452] Those who had left included fullers, weavers, dyers, drapers, glovers and skinners (*Rot. Hund.*, ii, 3). The wealthy townsmen were said to have failed to pay their share (RCHM, *Northampton*, 55; *VCH, Northamptonshire*, vol. III, 7, 26).

[453] PRO, SC 12/13/38; NRO, Royal Charter 29. The additional properties were almost entirely shops and stalls.

missing from the early rental were the 40+ properties of Gobion Manor, and the properties owned by the religious houses. At the Dissolution St Andrew's Priory owned about 100 urban properties, and St James' Abbey owned in excess of sixty. This seems to indicate over 500 properties and, depending upon the number of unrecorded properties, a population of about 3,000.[454] The heading of the early rental referred to the poverty of the town and indicated that some rents were *clara* and others were not. Occasionally properties were described as *vasta*, among them a shop in the Row in which oats, barley and dredge were sold, and a tenement near the castle.

Economic difficulties are perhaps indicated by the grant of murage in 1301. This was to last for five years and was therefore more extensive than the murage grant for three years made in 1224, and the two-year murage grant of 1251.[455] It has been suggested that the grant of 1301 was on a scale which indicated rebuilding rather than just repair; it may have indicated the enlargement of the town to include St Giles' Church and agricultural land.[456] In 1311 Northampton became one of the towns of Statute Merchant.[457]

In 1334 declining fortunes were becoming apparent. In that year Northampton's contribution to the lay subsidy was £27, which meant that it was not among the fifty highest urban contributors.[458] In the same year the town petitioned for a reduction of the fee farm, claiming that houses had fallen to the ground and their rents had accordingly been lost; those who served as bailiffs were made beggars as a result. The burgesses also asked for permission to hold a fair lasting from

---

454 RCHM, *Northampton*, 56.

455 *NBR*, vol. I, 36-7, 41-3, 58-60.

456 *NBR.*, vol. I, xxiv; *VCH, Northamptonshire*, vol. III, 30.

457 *NBR*, vol. I, xxv.

458 R.E. Glasscock (ed.), *The Lay Subsidy of 1334* (Oxford, 1975), 209, 218; RCHM, *Northampton*, 55.

Whitsuntide to 1 August, presumably hoping that this would increase the town's revenues. Their request hinted at the decline of the original fair, which occupied the whole of the month of November. No reduction in the farm was granted, and the council sanctioned only an eight-day fair. In 1337, however, possibly because of the town's continuing difficulties, a fair lasting for four weeks from the second Monday after Trinity was granted.[459]

No documentary evidence has been found which allows any assessment of the impact of the Black Death and subsequent outbreaks of plague upon Northampton. Problems in collecting the rents which went to the fee farm persisted, and in 1376 were mentioned in another petition to the king.[460] The poll tax of 1377 listed 1,477 taxable lay persons. These figures have been used to estimate a total population of 2,216 inhabitants, a figure seen as somewhat cautious, although there has been reluctance to put the total higher than 2,500. This would put Northampton 28th in terms of size of population.[461] The most recent estimate suggests a total of 2,810 inhabitants.[462]

In 1380 the last parliament held at Northampton took place. During this parliament the king stayed at Moulton and not at the castle, an indication perhaps that its condition had deteriorated.[463] An ordinance of c.1390-1400 allowed the mayor and chamberlains to lease out certain waste places from which no profits had accrued for some years, and which were allegedly occupied by 'thieves and other filthy

---

459 *VCH, Northamptonshire*, vol. III, 6, 19, 24; RCHM, *Northampton*, 55; *NBR.*, vol. I, xxvii, 66-8; Williams, *Saxon and Medieval Northampton*, 31.

460 *VCH, Northamptonshire*, vol. III, 19.

461 R.B. Dobson (ed.), *The Peasants' Revolt of 1381* (2nd edition, London, 1983), 56. In 1381 there were 1,518 taxpayers in Northampton (RCHM, *Northampton*, 55).

462 Dr Alan Dyer suggested this total at the conference 'Towns in Decline', held at the University of Birmingham 12-14 April 1996.

463 *VCH, Northamptonshire*, vol. III, 35.

persons'.[464] In 1400 a further grant of murage, this time for two years, was perhaps another hint of decay, although it did imply continuing concern for the upkeep of the walls. The legal powers granted to the mayor and commonalty in 1431 which enabled them to compel freeholders to maintain the pavements could also be seen either as a sign of deteriorating conditions or as an indication of civic determination to maintain the physical townscape – or both.[465]

A rental of St Andrew's Priory dating from 1403-4 listed 25 rents in decay. Some properties lacked tenants, three shops had fallen down, and one tenement had been destroyed by fire.[466] Documentary sources which allow any assessment of Northampton's population in the fifteenth century are lacking, but there is a little evidence which points to ongoing decline. In 1439-40 the names of some 60 alien householders at Northampton and of another 23 aliens who worked as servants in the town were listed in the alien subsidy assessment. Of these 83 people two had died, one was too poor to pay any tax, and 54 had moved. In 1449 only seven aliens were listed in the town, and ten years later only four.[467] No record survives of any reduction in its lay subsidy assessment granted to Northampton in the mid-fifteenth century. Other towns in the county saw their contributions reduced by varying amounts. Peterborough's 1334 assessment of £25 10s 6d was reduced by 52s, for example, and that of Towcester fell from £8 to £6.[468] It is unlikely that Northampton would have escaped the general malaise.

Proof that the town was indeed suffering economic difficulties may be seen in the remission of £20 from the fee farm for twenty years granted by Edward IV in 1462. In 1478 the period of remission was extended for a further twelve years, and it was

[464] *NBR*, vol. I, 251; *VCH, Northamptonshire*, vol. III, 30.
[465] *NBR*, vol. I, 72-4, 283-8.
[466] PRO, SC 6/948/18.
[467] PRO, E 179/155/80; E 179/155/88; E 179/155/95.
[468] PRO, E 179/155/105.

decreed that henceforth Northampton's mayors and escheators could take their oath of office in the town, instead of before the barons of the king's exchequer in London. This would remove the charges and expenses which the burgesses had long sustained in taking the oath in the capital.[469] That these charges were not insignificant can be seen in the mayor's accounts for the year 1378-9. Receipts totalled £8 12s 3d but expenditure amounted to £10 11s 8d, of which 45s went in the mayor's expenses travelling to and from London and during his stay in the capital, 56s 8d on gifts and 'remunerations' to justices and attorneys, and £5 on food and clothing for the clerk and *clientis*.[470]

In 1484 a further remission of the fee farm was granted by Richard III, upon hearing the 'lamentable information' provided by the mayor, bailiffs and burgesses. This had shown that in 'remote times' the inhabitants had prospered, that every quarter of the town had been inhabited and that scarcely any house had been unoccupied. As a result, the £120 fee farm could be paid out of rents, profits and revenues arising within the town without charges on their own goods. Recently, however, the town had fallen into ruin, and the inhabitants had fallen into poverty by the misfortunes and great charges and various expenses they sustained. As a result, almost half the town remained desolate and destroyed and destitute of fit persons to sustain the office of bailiffs. It was further noted that these officers had in particular sustained insupportable losses and had in recent years paid at least £53 6s 8d of their own goods beyond the yearly charges sustained by reason of their offices. Many burgesses who seemed fit to serve as bailiff were withdrawing their goods before they could be elected; within a few years no fit men would remain to bear office and the town would not be able to answer for any part of the fee farm.[471]

---

[469] *NBR*, vol. I, 91-2, 93-6.

[470] NRO, Royal Charter 28.

[471] *NBR*, vol. I, 97-101.

This plaintive chorus was echoed by many townsmen throughout England and their claims should not be accepted uncritically. By this period, moreover, it seems that towns may have come to expect financial relief from a new king just as in earlier years they had expected confirmation of their charters.[472] Their expectations were most likely to be fulfilled by kings who needed to cultivate support, and it was possibly because he sat somewhat uneasily upon the throne that in 1484 Richard III granted Northampton a remission of 50 marks for ever. In Winchester, however, it has been shown that the citizens' claims made in the mid-fifteenth century that 17 parish churches, 11 streets and 987 messuages had fallen into ruins during the last fifty years were not exaggerated and that they contained 'some remarkably precise elements'.[473]

The claims made at Northampton in 1484 that burgesses were withdrawing their goods from the town to avoid election as bailiff perhaps indicated divisions within the wealthiest section of the community. These dissensions and discords had become so apparent by 1489 that an Act of Parliament changed the borough constitution, with the result that from then onwards town government was in the hands of a closed body.[474] The charter of 1495 reflected the continuing decline of Northampton's trade by its mention of only two fairs in the town, one focusing on the feast of St George and the other on the feast of St Hugh; the duration of each fair was now limited to eight days.[475] From at least 1498 Coventry usurped the place of Northampton as the periodic venue for provincial chapters of the Black Monks.[476]

---

[472] S.H. Rigby, 'Urban decline in the later middle ages: the reliability of the non-statistical evidence', *Urban History Yearbook* (1984), 45.

[473] Keene, *Winchester in the Later Middle Ages*, vol. I, 96-8.

[474] *NBR*, vol. I, 101; *VCH, Northamptonshire*, vol. III, 8-9.

[475] *NBR*, vol. I, 104; *VCH, Northamptonshire*, vol. III, 24.

[476] Phythian-Adams, *Desolation*, 21.

In 1503-4 the royal rental of properties in Northampton was renewed.[477] Many of the tenements listed in the rental dating from the reign of Edward I can be recognised but there are also indications of change. In Swinewell Street three tenements had been incorporated into a barn; a lane behind a capital tenement in Kingswell Street had been enclosed; five shops in the old Glovers' Row had been enclosed and now formed one tenement; a former hall near the Franciscan friary had become a stable; a capital tenement (perhaps in Gold Street) and two others in Newlands had become gardens. The fact that the names of current tenants could not be given for a sizeable number of properties may perhaps be interpreted as a further indication of decline. In the area next to the castle, for example, no tenants were named for any of the nine tenements listed, and only one tenant was named for seven properties in Holy Sepulchre Street. No tenants were named for any of the six shops in the Hosiers' Row. Many of the major town houses formerly held by wealthy townsmen were now held by local gentlemen and a number now served as inns.

This evidence for a reduction in population between the late thirteenth and early sixteenth centuries was reflected to a certain extent in the fortunes of the parish churches. Of the nine recorded in 1200 that of St Bartholomew had declined in status and become a chapel apparently before the Feudal Aid of 1428, which gave the number of parishes in the town as eight. Between that date and 1535 the number of parishes remained the same, although the value of the churches of St Edmund and of St Michael decreased, the latter by more than half.[478] It was not until after the Reformation, however, that the churches of St Michael, St Gregory, St Edmund and St Mary fell out of use.

---

[477] NRO, Royal Charter 29.

[478] *VCH, Northamptonshire*, vol. III, 55; Williams, *Saxon and Medieval Northampton*, 48. The value of St Gregory's remained much the same, that of St Mary's increased slightly, the values of All Saints', St Giles' and Holy Sepulchre increased more substantially, while the value of St Peter's, which drew income from the dependent chapelries of Kingsthorpe and Upton, increased from £26 13s 4d to £41 6s 8d.

In 1514 Henry VIII granted Northampton a permanent remission of £22 of the fee farm, together with claims to all arrears then due and owing; this reduction was backdated to September 1508.[479] In 1516 the 'greatest part of the town' was said to have been destroyed by fire.[480] The subsidy assessment of 1524 listed some 480 taxpayers, presumably the heads of households.[481] A total population of between 2,800 and 3,000 derived from these figures has recently been increased to 3,100 and Northampton therefore featured among the 'growing' towns, its population having increased by 290 since 1377, when the population was 2,810. In 1524-5 Northampton's nearest rivals were Coventry with 725 taxpayers, and Leicester with about 400 taxpayers.[482] A ranking of 21st has been suggested for Northampton in the 1520s, with the town heading the group between 3,000 and 4,000 in size.[483]

In 1524 William B[and] fishmonger, assessed on goods valued at £95 was the wealthiest taxpayer in Northampton. The mayor was assessed on goods valued at £66 13s 4d, and a grocer was assessed on goods valued at £60; seven burgesses were assessed on goods worth £50, and five on goods worth £40 or more. This is not suggestive of great personal wealth. The highest taxpayer in Brackley was assessed on goods worth £100; at Kettering two men were assessed on goods of this value. In 1526 the mayor of Northampton, together with nine eminent townsmen, certified to royal officials that none of the inhabitants of the town or its liberties had lands, rents, annuities or other yearly profits worth £50 or more.[484] How much credence should be given to this claim is debatable. In 1535 the

---

479 *NBR*, vol. I, 113-15.

480 *VCH, Northamptonshire*, vol. III, 31.

481 PRO, E 179/155/124.

482 Dyer, 'Northampton in 1524', 73. In note 2 he suggested that if a third of the population were excluded from the assessment, then the total would be 3,240. *Idem*, 'Towns in Decline'.

483 Phythian-Adams, *Desolation*, 12.

484 PRO, E 179/155/152.

bequests of one of the signatories included £67 to making the new market cross and £10 to mending the highway in St James' End.[485]

In that year, because of the great ruin and decay of the town, the mayor and burgesses were empowered by parliament to appropriate and rebuild any houses which the tenants and landlords failed to repair. If they failed to do so, then anyone who pleased might rebuild the houses and so acquire possession of them and of the land on which they stood.[486] A more or less contemporary description spoke of 'notable decay first of the houses, whereof part belonged to the religious houses which were lately suppressed which were evil repairers of their lands and part to the gentlemen of the country who extort as much rent as they can and leave all repairs to the tenants who now let their housing fall in ruin to the great deformity of the town'.[487] Leland visited Northampton at some point in the years 1535-43 and noted that the old houses of Northampton were stone-built but that new houses were of timber. He spoke of a 'faire' suburb outside the South Gate, and a smaller suburb beyond the West Gate which contained 'a very pratie house *ex lapide polite quadrato.*' Large and fair walls of similar stone encompassed St James' Abbey.[488] In this respect the abbey was in better repair than St Andrew's Priory, whose stone walls in 1538 were described as 'very ruinous'.[489]

Conclusion

Much can be learned about late medieval Northampton from the documentary sources alone. It is possible to discuss the town's economic and social

---

[485] PRO, PROB 11/26 27 Hogen; extracts quoted in Serjeantson and Longden, 'Parish Churches of Northamptonshire', 376.

[486] *VCH, Northamptonshire*, vol. III, 31.

[487] RCHM, *Northampton*, 57.

[488] Leland, *Itinerary*, 7-9.

[489] PRO, E 315/399, f. 254.

development in some detail, and to address such issues as its ranking in the urban hierarchy of its region, its relationships with neighbouring towns, and its links with the countryside. The analysis takes on new meaning, however, when the historical and archaeological evidence is collated systematically, as was done by the project. The problems and possibilities of an interdisciplinary approach emerged clearly in the study of Northampton. On some issues, the two sets of data proved complementary; on others, the evidence of one discipline urged a more cautious interpretation by the second; on occasion, the documentary and the material evidence appeared contradictory.

The archaeological and the historical evidence was broadly in agreement when attempts were made to establish demographic trends. The taxation records suggested that the population of Northampton, having perhaps peaked at c.5,000 in the late twelfth century, approached 3,000 in the late fourteenth century, and was little higher in the early sixteenth century. Archaeological excavations indicated that the town was most densely occupied in the thirteenth century and experienced shrinkage in the later medieval period, with occupation ceasing at sites in the south-eastern quarter but with demand for land in the commercial core remaining high. The material evidence thus provided an understanding of the spatial distribution of decline which was largely absent from the documents, although detailed analysis of the two rentals would certainly yield some corroborative information.

At Northampton, the use of standing buildings as indicators of fluctuations in population and wealth was hampered by the paucity of surviving structures. Of the nine medieval churches, for example, only three remain. Records for all the churches are available to the historian, although some churches are better documented than others. However, much of the evidence is derived from probate records, and thus dates from the second half of the fifteenth century and the early sixteenth century. This is a common problem with the documentary sources, which not infrequently relate to one particular year. Archaeology is better served, with long sequences of occupation and development often revealed. The differences between the two sets of data help to explain the varying interpretations of St Peter's Church. The surviving structure reflects its origins as a religious house attached to the castle and with limited parochial functions. The wills indicate that by the second half of the fifteenth century it functioned as a 'normal' parish church with a relatively small congregation of artisans and craftsmen. The evidence of the wills also underlines the problems inherent in using the size and splendour of a church as an indicator of population growth within the parish. All Saints' played a particular role in the civic life of late medieval Northampton and housed a number of the most prestigious guilds. It benefited from the generosity of wealthy men who lived elsewhere in the town but who chose to worship and to be buried there.

The two sets of data allowed the identification of occupational areas. The tanning quarter in the south-western quarter of the town emerged clearly both in the documentary sources and in the archaeological excavations. A 'genteel' residential quarter in the parish of St Giles was attested in both disciplines. However, evidence for metal-working in the western area of the town was discovered only by the archaeologists. This activity has left no record in the documents, which identified metal-workers only in the eastern part of Northampton. The pins, lace tags, and other items they produced were not mentioned in the historical sources, which were rarely concerned with items of such small value. No references to pottery have been found in the surviving wills. Yet these are the finds which bulk so large in archaeological excavations and which perhaps reflect the life of the urban community more closely than do the silver plate and fine clothing mentioned in bequests, an indication that archaeology has the potential to reveal more about the poorer members of society. Environmental evidence including animal bones and plant remains can provide much information about medieval diet. Corroborative evidence can be found in the documentary sources, from the lists of the different types of fish traded in the town, for example, and from the kitchens furnished with spits indicative of the consumption of expensive joints of meat.

Both the material and the historical data were searched for evidence of Northampton's marketing networks in the late medieval period. The archaeological evidence was largely based on an analysis of ceramic assemblages. These were dominated by local wares but included regional imports from Oxfordshire, Warwickshire and London, and some fragments of Dutch floor tiles. The documents provided a more comprehensive understanding of the town's trading links, despite the lack of borough court rolls which always prove such a valuable source of information. It was nevertheless possible to suggest the nature of the contacts between Northampton and its rural hinterland, to understand something of the interaction between the top-ranking county town and the towns lower down the urban hierarchy, and to appreciate the strong pull of Coventry, the regional capital, and of London, the dominant metropolis.

In sum, the integration of both documentary and archaeological material presents both problems and challenges. Sometimes it raises more questions than it answers. But it is still provides the best means by which the complexities of late medieval urban development can be investigated. In the case of Northampton, these two papers have created a wide-ranging study of the community in a period when the town confirmed its position as one of the major regional towns of the East Midlands.